PLUMBED: Tired of being soaked when you call a plumber? Here's everything you need to know to keep your plumbing drip-free and flowing from kitchen to bath.

WIRED: Shockingly easy step-by-step instructions for installing and repairing lighting fixtures, switches, outlets, lamps and anything else electrical.

NAILED: Don't get hammered by the cost of carpentry! You can fix nearly everything made of wood—doors, cabinets, paneling, windowsills, molding, decks, garages....

PLUGGED: Cold dryer? Warm refrigerator? You can make over half of all needed home appliance repairs at one-tenth the cost of a service call.

REVVED: Drive your transportation costs down through the floorboards by following our unique preventative maintenance checklists and comprehensive guide to easy car repairs.

HARLEQUIN ULTIMATE GUIDES ™

I CAN FIX THAT

BY SUSIE TOMPKINS

Harlequin Books

TORONTO • NEW YORK • LONDON
AMSTERDAM • PARIS • SYDNEY • HAMBURG
STOCKHOLM • ATHENS • TOKYO • MILAN
MADRID • WARSAW • BUDAPEST • AUCKLAND

ISBN 0-373-80508-X

I Can Fix That

Copyright © 1996 by TD MEDIA INC.

Design by Figure 5 Design
Interior artwork by David Smith

This edition published by arrangement with Harlequin Books S.A.

® and TM are trademarks of the publisher. Trademarks indicated with ® are registered in the United States Patent and Trademark Office, the Canadian Trade Marks Office and in other countries.

Printed in U.S.A.

CONTENTS

INTRODUCTION

My father's domain was the corner of the basement he called his workshop. It was the place he proudly kept his tools hanging neatly and his hardware organized and stored in little wooden boxes he lovingly built with his own hands. Once he told me that it was the only place in the world where he knew exactly where everything was and I could tell it made him happy. He loved to take care of our home spending his weekends and vacations keeping everything in tip-top shape.

His philosophy was a simple one. "Why should I pay somebody else for something I can do myself," he said as I watched him fix a toilet or repair a broken window. Years later, after spending a lot of money for work I could have done myself I took that philosophy to heart and started taking care of business around the house on my own. And believe it or not—you can too!

The True Facts Something like 60% to 80% of the cost of home repair goes to paying the expert for his time. Materials make up the balance. It's obvious that there are a lot of jobs that a beginner shouldn't tackle. But all of it can be learned and how skilled you become is up to you. Even at the simplest level, it's not hard to see that there's a good reason for learning enough about your home and its operating systems to do basic maintenance and repair—saving your hard-earned money. The corporate giants have seen the light and jumped on the home repair bandwagon in a big way. They've realized that more people are willing to "do it" themselves and so they are working overtime to market products and new technology in attractive packaging complete with easy to understand instructions and 1-800 Help Lines.

Home repair and maintenance is becoming simpler in concept and is becoming even easier in execution. All it takes are a few tools, a bit of confidence, and the patience to follow the necessary steps. **Let's do it!**

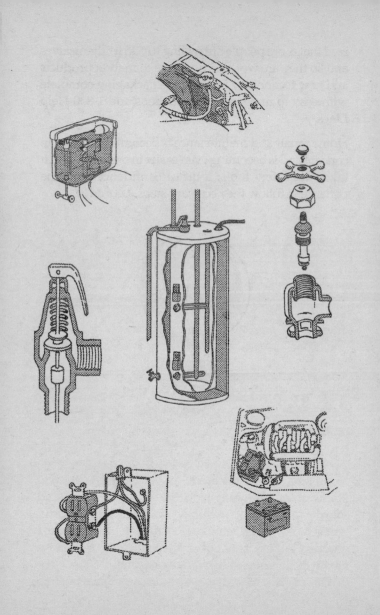

I CAN FIX THAT— PLUMBED

FIXING SINKS MEANS WEARING MINKS

Did you ever stop and wonder why your trusty plumber drives a better car than you do no matter how he dresses to go under your sink? It's easy—like all the trades—labor is the biggest part of the bill. Take it from me, do-it-yourself plumbing can save you a fortune and, as usual, I learned the hard way.

A kindly old pipefitter once took pity on me when he saw my mascara running after he handed over a giant bill for fixing a washer in my bathroom sink. Maybe he was about to retire or something but as he sat at my kitchen table waiting for me to sign the check, he looked me in the eye and said, "Ya know, Mrs. Tompkins, forgive my French but all you really need to know about plumbing is 'waste' flows downhill and payday's on Friday." Actually "waste" is a less colorful version of what he actually said but you get the point. I nodded politely, looked for the valium and went on about the insanity I call my daily routine.

Then, late one afternoon, I was in the kitchen peeling

carrots and watching "Oprah" when my four year old came running up and said, "Mommy, somebody 'made' on the bathroom ceiling." Now, between the kids, the cats, and the dog, someone has 'made' on nearly every square foot of my house, but this was definitely a new one.

When I followed him into the bathroom, I got that feeling in the pit of my stomach that says, "We're eating macaroni and cheese for three weeks." On my freshly painted white ceiling was an ugly brownish stain. I dashed upstairs to the bathroom above it, and found that the base of the toilet was wet. I beeped my plumber, who docked his yacht, drove over to the house, and told me the bad news was that the wax seal needed to be replaced. The good news was that there wasn't any dry rot so the floor didn't need to be redone. An hour later, we were dry but $120 poorer.

I'd nearly forgotten about the trauma a couple of weeks later when I happened down the wrong aisle of the hardware store. Right in front of me, I spotted a wax ring just like the one my plumber had put under my toilet. The price: $2.43. Suddenly, I saw red—and about 14 other colors. Just to be sure it wasn't some mistake, I grabbed a store employee. He not only told me that the price was right, but that replacing the seal involved little more than turning off the water, loosening some bolts, and lifting the toilet.

I rushed out of the store ready to strangle the plumber, but, by the time I got the kids strapped into the car, I realized it wasn't really his fault. I was the one who spent/wasted the $117.57 I could have put toward my full-length mink and some Dunkin' Doughnuts for George and the kids. I finally understood what the ancient pipefitter told me so long ago in the kitchen—basic plumbing's not that hard, it only seems that way. Right then and there, I made a vow to myself. I turned to my brood and said, "Meet the new Tompkins family plumber—me."

THE HARDWARE JUNGLE

One of nature's strangest optical phenomena, along with mirages and the Northern Lights, is the indisputable fact that a dress that looks sensational in the store dressing room looks hideous when you get it home. A related phenomenon is that a washer, a piece of pipe, or any other plumbing doo-dad that looks like exactly what you need in the hardware store will turn out to be the wrong piece when you get it home. Since you want to avoid repeat trips when you've got a plumbing emergency, here's a few shopping tips:

Take the pieces you need to replace to the store and match them side-by-side with new pieces.

Find a hardware store that has washers, pieces of pipe, and other parts in individual bins but also sells complete kits of parts in plastic bags and whole replacement units. The logic is simple, if you just need a widget you don't want to be forced to buy the framitz and the whatchacallit. If you buy a kit, you'll probably be purchasing parts you don't need and once you open the bag, the kit may not be returnable. On the other hand, if you need the whole pie it's nice to know you can get it.

Two opinions are better than one, so ask for help from a store employee. At the very least, you have someone to blame if you're both wrong.

GO WITH THE FLOW:

UNDERSTANDING YOUR HOME'S PLUMBING SYSTEM

Water comes into your house from one of two places, (assuming there aren't any leaks in the roof) your private well or a city water main. In either case, a single service pipe buried below the frost line runs into your home where it is then distributed to all the places it's needed.

If your service comes from the city water corporation, a water meter to calculate usage is most often installed just inside the basement. (Although occasionally you will find it in a meter pit just outside the house.) On either side of the water meter you'll find two large shutoff valves, sort of like the ones you see behind the actors in movies that take place on ships.

The valve closest to the basement wall is usually called the meter stop or the street side valve and the one on the other side is the house main valve. Turning the valve one way shuts the water off, turning it the other turns the water on. Simple, yes, but not so easy to remember in an emergency when water's spurting and kids are screaming. Get to know the location of the house main valve and how it works because, in an emergency, shutting off the main in time can save you hundreds of dollars in replacement and damage repair.

From this point, imagine a tree with its trunk and many branches growing up and spreading out and you'll get a picture of how your system moves through your house. There are two basic parts of the system: The Supply Side, which brings fresh water into your home and The Drainage Side which takes soiled water away.

THE SUPPLY SIDE

COLD WATER SUPPLY LINES From the meter, a single cold water line called the trunk line moves up the basement wall and across a central beam of your house. From the trunk are, of course, branches, at necessary intervals. They carry the cold water where it's needed in the house to service sinks, toilets, bathtubs, showers and washing machines, etc.

HOT WATER SUPPLY LINES At some point, a cold water line will branch off the trunk and feed into your hot water heater to fill the tank. Another line carrying the hot water will rise from the water heater and join the cold water line as it runs along the central beam. It's called the hot water trunk line and provides the feed to sinks, showers, bathtubs, dishwashers, and washing machines.

THE DRAINAGE SIDE

DRAINAGE LINES OK. We've got the water into your house, now we've got to get rid it after it's been used. This is the job of the drainage system and it's in the drainage lines that a lot of problems in a plumbing system arise. The drainage lines are a series of one or more large vertical pipes that run through centrally located positions in your house called stacks to which all the horizontal drains (from the toilet, sinks, washing machines, etc.) are attached. The system drains all the soiled water to a large sewer service pipe beneath your house that feeds into the main sewer system.

Unlike the supply system, in which the water is fed by pressure, the drainage system is dependent on gravity to do its work. Therefore, it's crucial that the horizontal drain pipes are installed at what is called the correct pitch (or fall, or slope) so that the water flows downward at a speed insuring the removal of solid waste. If the pitch is too shallow, the water will move slowly and the solid matter will clog the lines. If the pitch is too great, the water will move faster than the waste which will also cause the lines to clog. Correct pitch is considered to be a fall of 1/8th to 1/4 of an inch per foot. If your drainage system seems sluggish you can find out what the pitch is by placing your handy two-foot level (See: Nailed) on a horizontal drain pipe, raising it so the bubble is level and measuring the distance between the level and the pipe to see if it's in the correct range.

TRAPS All fixtures (sinks, toilets, showers, bathtubs, dishwashers, washing machines) that require a drain also require a trap. The trap is that "U" shaped pipe under the sink or behind the washing machine. The trap is one of the most important elements of a plumbing system because it allows soiled water to pass through it, but stops evil smelling and sometimes dangerous sewer gases from coming back into the house. It can also become clogged in the process, but we'll get to that later. It works by holding a certain amount of water in the "U." After the sink or toilet has been drained, the water acts as a seal that the sewer gases can't penetrate. It's simple and it works like a charm, as long as it's vented properly.

VENTING LINES After fixture traps, properly installed venting lines are essential to the drainage system working well. The most common venting lines are vertical extensions of the drain lines themselves that extend up and connect to a main vent that comes up through the roof of your house. Without good venting nothing will work like it should, toilets won't flush properly, drains choke and high pressure appliances like washing machines will overflow. But most importantly, drains that are vented badly will siphon off water from the trap and sewer gas will run amok through your house .

PART TWO

WHAT TO DO IN AN EMERGENCY

I don't know about you, but it's always been my feeling that emergencies should be scheduled like trips to the dentist. They're not something you look forward to, but at least you've got time to prepare. Of course, that's not the way it works, so when things go wrong we resort to the only alternative usually left—panic. Why panic? Because we're not prepared. There's nothing more frightening than watching helplessly as water gushes out of places it's not supposed to while the kids are screaming and the dog is barking. Let's face it, this atmosphere is not conducive to rational thought—unless you've realized, in a rational moment, that something like this could happen and you have a plan.

KNOW YOUR SYSTEM

The first part of the plan is to take that little tour of your plumbing system so you know where everything is and have a general idea of how it's all connected. Start in the basement in whatever corner the water meter resides. Trace your way through your home, noting the places where other shutoff valves hide. (Under your sink, behind the toilet or washing machine, above the water heater.) Because the first rule in a plumbing emergency is SHUT IT OFF. But the key here is to shut it off *behind* the leak. There's no sense in turning off the shutoff valves under the sink if the leak is in the basement. There's also no point in shutting off the house main to fix the bathroom toilet.

WHAT TO DO AFTER YOU SHUT IT OFF

No matter how soggy everything seems once the water stops flowing, it's a lot less soggy than it would have been if you ran around like a chicken with your head cut off wondering where the little valves were. Take heart, once you've stemmed the tide you've got a little breathing room, not only to survey the damage, but to see what you can do about it. Whether or not the problem is something you can fix yourself, either temporarily or permanently, or whether you have to call in an expert.

THEY'RE PIPES FOR CRYING OUT LOUD— WHY DON'T THEY LAST FOREVER?

Plumbing emergencies that can do serious damage to your bank account most often come from burst pipes. Luckily there is some damage control you can do until professional help arrives.

Pipes crack or split for a lot of reasons: they freeze because they're improperly insulated; they're the wrong size for the volume of water that has to pass

CHERRY RED TO THE RESCUE

Any woman who's sat in the passenger seat of a car for three hours while her husband searches for a wedding reception knows that men have two firm rules: never ask directions and never label anything. The first can be downright annoying, but the second can be disastrous if a kitchen pipe erupts like Old Faithful and threatens to turn your kitchen into an indoor pool.

My friend, Sally, came up with a great solution using that old standby—nail polish. She located the main shutoff valve and wrote "main" in red nail polish on the pipe. On the handle, she drew an arrow in red nail polish to indicate what direction was off, and an arrow in green nail polish to indicate what direction was on. She did the same thing on every other shutoff valve in the house. Sally says she sleeps better at night.

through them; they contain factory defects or, sometimes, they just wear out after years of use. The methods of emergency repair are similar for each problem.

FROZEN PIPES Pipes freeze because they often run through exterior walls and are not insulated properly against cold weather or are exposed to cold drafts. A little ice cube forms in the pipe and expands until it puts enough pressure on the wall of the pipe to make it burst. It's easy to tell if a pipe is frozen, you turn on the faucet and either a trickle comes out or nothing at all. Trace the run to the exterior wall and feel the pipe. Often you can tell where the freeze is before it bursts because it's the coldest part of the pipe.

Use Your Hairdryer Leave a faucet turned on near the frozen pipe. Take your hairdryer and pass it back and forth along the freeze until it thaws and water runs freely through the faucet. Get some insulation and wrap the pipe immediately so it won't happen again and count yourself lucky.

BURST PIPES If the frozen pipe has already burst, drain the system by shutting off the valve behind the break so no more water will run through it after the pipe is thawed. Use your trusty hairdryer to thaw it out and then survey the damage. Here are some emergency fixes. (See **Part Three: Tools of the Trade** to get a grip on the tools and materials you'll need.)

Really Temporary This is the one you use if you're really in a jam. Take the inner tube and the hose clamps I suggest you include in your tool kit. This is where preparation pays off. Cut a piece of inner tube several inches longer than the split or leak. Wrap it around the pipe several times and tighten the hose clamps on either side of the leak. While it isn't permanent and won't stop the leak entirely it'll get you through until help arrives.

Rubber Repair Coupling These handy little items are available at hardware stores and plumbing supply houses in several sizes. If you have a store handy, and have the time to get there, they are a good solution because they are relatively permanent.

Once the pipe is empty and dry, take a wire brush or some gritty sandpaper and clean the pipe all around. Then fit the rubber sleeve around the pipe so that the seam is opposite the split or leak. Fit the hinged metal collar over the sleeve, tighten it in place and you're done.

Epoxy Patches After the pipe is dry, clean it well with sandpaper and alcohol. Mix the epoxy according to the manufacturer's instructions. Once mixed, you'll have about 15 minutes to work with the stuff. Put the putty all around the pipe until it covers the leak. Take a wet rag and feather out the ends until they are smooth and blend seamlessly with the pipe. Epoxy takes a full 24 hours to set up and cure but you should be able to turn the water back on at low pressure in 6 to 8 hours. Patience is the key here, wait the full 24 hours before you bring the pressure up to normal or you'll be doing the whole thing all over again. If done correctly, this constitutes a permanent fix.

SUSIE'S HELPFUL HINTS

If you're going to be gone from the house for an extended period during the winter months, drain your plumbing system. If it's just a few days, turn on a faucet just enough for a trickle to escape. Running water won't freeze.

PART THREE

TOOLS OF THE TRADE:

WHAT YOU NEED FOR SIMPLE PLUMBING REPAIRS

WHAT'S IN THE BOX? One of the things that's really fun about taking on "Fix-It" tasks is building up a set of tools to make the work easier. Over the years, trial and error (and smart engineers) have produced specialized tools that turn an impossible task into a breeze. It's true and really worth the effort if you're serious about taking care of business on your own.

(See the **Glossary** section for whats and whys.)

HERE'S WHAT I CARRY IN MINE

- ☐ adjustable wrench
- ☐ box wrench
- ☐ bucket (metal or plastic)
- ☐ drain auger
- ☐ epoxy repair kit
- ☐ hacksaw
- ☐ hairdryer
- ☐ hammer
- ☐ hose clamps
- ☐ inner tube

- ☐ leather gloves
- ☐ locking pliers
- ☐ mat knife
- ☐ open-end wrench
- ☐ Phillips screwdriver
- ☐ pipe joint compound
- ☐ pipe wrench
- ☐ rubber coupling
- ☐ rubber gloves

- ☐ rubber mallet
- ☐ sink plunger
- ☐ slotted screwdriver
- ☐ spud and basin wrenches
- ☐ toilet auger
- ☐ toilet plunger
- ☐ waterproof grease
- ☐ wire brush

PART FOUR

PLUMBING PROBLEMS:

IN THE KITCHEN
IN THE BATHROOM
IN THE BASEMENT

Following are some "Fix-Its" you can take on with confidence, get results and learn some of the skills necessary for taking on larger projects. They're kind of all over your house—but then, so is your plumbing.

FAUCETS—THE THINGS THAT GO DRIP IN THE NIGHT

Anyone who's ever owned a dog whistle knows it's a biological fact that certain species can't hear certain sounds. You have to be married to know one example of this rule is that husbands are totally deaf to drips. To me, on the other hand, a drop of water hitting the bathtub stopper in the middle of the night sounds like a percussionist slamming two cymbals together. If I nudged George awake in the old days, his first words will be, "What drip?" My only recourse was to drag him into the bathroom and put his head under the spout. For that, I would receive an "I'll get to it this weekend."

I didn't realize until I decided to take up plumbing that a ten-cent piece of rubber could stop those water drops from playing the bongos all night long. If you can screw in a light bulb, you can replace a washer. The benefits are enormous—you save on your water bill, you get to sleep at night, and best of all, your husband can spend the weekend on one of those truly challenging household duties, watching the kids.

FIXING FAUCETS The world is full of faucets. They come in lots of shapes and sizes but when the dust clears there are really two different kinds. Both of them may seem confusing and difficult to repair, but I figured it out and so can you.

Fixing most of the little things that go wrong with faucets simply requires patience, the right tools and a good memory. Why a good memory, you may ask? When you take a faucet apart you'll know why. There are a lot of little pieces and they all have to go back in the right order or you might as well have spent the afternoon playing bridge.

The two basic varieties of faucets are STEM and SEAT AND SPRING.

The Seat and Spring styles have come to be known as "washerless." Rather than using a stem valve, the Seat and Spring faucet uses a "cartridge" that aligns on tabs and slides into place. They are really great because they last a long time and are easy to fix. They come in kits with complete and easy to understand directions. Washerless faucets come in "single lever" and the familiar two handle variety. (Note: The highest quality and longest-lasting sink valves you can buy are called Ceramic Disk Valves. They are in the "washerless" family but use ceramic or heavy duty plastic disks that seal tightly. Replacements come in kit form and are easy to work on.)

We're going to spend most of our time on Stem faucets because they don't come in kits and the fixing process is a great way to learn some basic plumbing skills.

STEM FAUCETS The stem in the stem faucet is what regulates the flow of water through the faucet. Turning the knob makes the stem go up or down. When the stem goes up water flows, when the stem goes down water doesn't. The assembly has safeguards against leaks, such as washers and packing. However, we live in an imperfect world and things wear out.

If your faucet leaks at the spout the culprit is the seat washer at the bottom of the stem assembly or the seat valve. If you see water leaking where the faucet meets the sink it's the packing in the packing (or bonnet) nut that needs replacement.

You know what to do first. Turn off the water at the shutoff valve below the sink and turn on the faucet to drain the pipe.

Replacing The Stem Washer Then, and this is what varies from style to style, you need to remove the decorative cap that covers the screw that holds the handle in place. It might take a second but you'll figure it out. Take a screwdriver, remove the screw and lift off the handle. (Place all the parts in a little box or on a dish so you don't lose them.) Sometimes you have to use some real force to knock it off.

Next, take your wrench and unscrew the packing nut. Lift out the stem.

At the bottom of the stem you'll see the stem washer attached by a screw or a top hat-shaped diaphragm. To replace the washer, remove the screw and replace the washer with an *exact* duplicate. If you aren't sure, take the worn washer to the hardware store and match it. While you're there get a couple of extras and pick up a bag of assorted sizes. To replace the diaphragm take off the old one and put on the new one.

Before you reassemble the faucet, coat the moving parts with waterproof grease. This will help prevent leaks, make it work more smoothly and make the faucet easier to remove next time.

Put it back together in the reverse order you took it apart and you're ready to turn the water back on and wash your hands—unless it still leaks.

If the faucet still leaks after you've replaced the stem washer the problem is the seat valve and, while it's a little trickier and requires a couple of extra tools, it's still worth the effort of doing it yourself.

Replacing The Valve Seat The valve seat can be resurfaced or replaced. To replace it you need a seat wrench and a new seat valve which you can get at the hard-

FAUCET

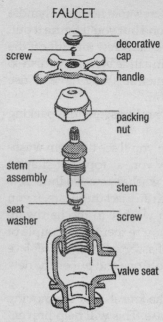

ware store. After you've removed the stem, insert the seat wrench and turn it counterclockwise to remove the old valve seat. Coat the new valve seat in pipe joint compound, push it firmly onto the stem wrench and screw it into place.

Resurfacing The Valve Seat Of course, sometimes, especially in older faucets the valve seat can't be removed from the seat valve because it's built in. (Don't you just love the terminology. No wonder most people think the people who know hardware are gods.) This is still no problem, it just requires a tool called a seat cutter. The seat cutter fits into the valve seat and grinds away the corrosion that's been tearing up your washers. You can tell when you're done when the cutter turns smoothly. Replace the washer on the stem valve, if you haven't done it already, and put it all back together.

Repacking The Packing In The Packing Nut (No It's Not A Song) If water is seeping around the point where the faucet meets the sink you've got to replace the packing in the packing nut. Packing comes in several forms and it'll be clear which one is yours once you remove the packing nut. It might be a packing washer, in which case you pop the old washer out with a screwdriver and pop the new one back in. If it's an "O" ring, snap it on the same way you took it off. Self-forming packing is a little more labor intensive. You have to unwind the old packing and rewind new stuff in its place. Add enough to fill the packing nut and about half again as much. When you retighten the packing nut the packing will compress, making a solid seal.

UNCLOGGING A DRAIN I don't know about you, but George and I decided to have children so someone could support us in our old age. So education is big around our household (can you say, "investment banking?"), and we encourage our children's curiosity. However, there are limits— such as the day the two youngest decided to see how many pennies they could drop down the bathroom sink. I cleaned out the trap beneath the sink, but some of the adventurous pennies had evidently maneuvered their way to the basement pipes, where they teamed up with wads of hair and who knows what else, to form a clog Draino couldn't budge.

Roto-Rooter was busy, so I dialed numbers from the Yellow Pages until I found a man who came right over. Even though the house call cost me $60, it turned out to be my lucky day. This man took me down to the basement to see how his snake worked. (No, not that kind of snake!) He showed me that fitted on the waste pipe which carried water out of the house were a number of caps that could be removed with a wrench. He removed one of the caps, then took out his snake, which turned out to be a long piece of thick wire with a little whirly thing on the end. He threaded the snake into the pipe, twisted it around for a while, and pop, the clog was gone. He told me I could do the same thing myself, and he even sold me a 25-foot-long snake for $5.49.

I don't have a clue as to why he taught me to do this, but I've used the snake dozens of times since. (Come to think of it, I have given his name to 426 of my closest friends.)

TOILETS—YOU NEED THEM

All it takes to realize how essential an item the old "euphemism" is, is to be without it while you wait several hours (or days) for the plumber. Did you know that the toilet is responsible for more than half the water use in the average home? That's a lot of water

> ⚠ **SUSIE'S WARNING:**
> If your drain is really clogged, never, and I repeat never, use lye-based or other caustic drain cleaners to free it. Why? If the clog is that severe they won't do the job anyway, and you or somebody else is going to have to remove the trap to work on it— and guess what? All those nasty chemicals are going to be sitting there waiting to spill all over your hands and arms when you take the trap apart.

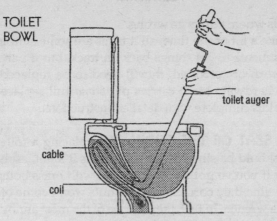

TOILET
BOWL

toilet auger

cable

coil

when things are working perfectly and it also means that leaks and other problems are sending thousands of wasted gallons down the drain each year. The fact is, a toilet is a very simple mechanical device and most of its pieces (and the problems) are right in front of your eyes once you lift the lid on the tank.

Take the hands-on approach, which I recommend highly, and flush the toilet with the lid off so you can watch it in action and see what happens.

This is what you'll see if everything's in order.

When you push the handle on the toilet the lever inside lifts the stopper ball out of the flush valve seat at the bottom of the tank. This allows the water to pour into the toilet bowl and (are you ready?) *flush* it out. As the water level in the tank falls, the float ball drops with it, opening the ball-cock valve and letting water from the inlet pipe refill the tank and bowl. This causes the float ball to rise until the ballcock valve closes, shutting off the water. That's about it and in the tank is where things go wrong.

Quite a lot of the time, all it takes are some simple adjustments to get things back on track, but if parts are worn or corroded, they'll need to be replaced. Your hardware store carries parts *and* full replacement kits complete with detailed instructions.

THE SEAT OF THE PROBLEM Replacing a toilet seat should be simple, but sometimes it's not, especially if you've got an older model with brass bolts. Over time they corrode and the nuts won't come off with a wrench. In fact, they do one of the most annoying things in all of "Fix-Itdom," they just sit there and turn. When this happens it's time for the hacksaw and some electrical or duct tape. Use the tape to protect the bowl from scratches, grab the hacksaw and go to work. It'll take you a while, but the good news is that most replacement seats use plastic nuts and bolts and you'll never have to do it again. The key to using a hacksaw effectively is not to hurry and let the tool do the work. Light pressure will actually get the job done faster than trying to be Queen Kong.

LEAKY TOILETS If the tank of your toilet is mounted on the bowl, as many are, eventually the connection between the bowl and the tank will begin to leak. To stop it, first drain the tank by shutting off the valve and flushing the toilet. When the tank is empty you'll see the heads of the bolts that secure the tank to the bowl. Get a friend and make her your assistant by giving her a screwdriver. Have her hold the head of the bolt inside the tank in place while you slowly and gently

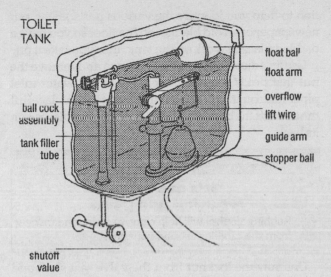

TOILET
TANK

float ball
float arm

overflow

ball cock
assembly

lift wire

guide arm

tank filler
tube

stopper ball

shutoff
value

tighten the nut underneath with a wrench. If a friend
isn't available get one of the kids.

> **IMPORTANT:** Whenever you tighten nuts
> on porcelain fixtures such as toilets or sinks,
> do it carefully and slowly. Over-tightening
> can crack the tank, bowl or basin resulting
> in an expensive replacement.

If this doesn't do it you'll have to remove the bolts
and replace the rubber washers. Do them one at time
so the tank doesn't shift off its cushion, which could
cause leaks that aren't already there.

If the tank still leaks, the problem is likely to be the
flush valve assembly and to fix it you're going to have
to take the tank off. Isn't this exciting? (See the illustra-

tion to help you identify the various parts.) First, put newspaper or an old blanket on the floor so you have a padded place to work on the tank after you take it off.

Use an adjustable wrench to loosen and remove the nut that holds the ball-cock shaft to the water inlet pipe. Take out the bolts that hold the tank in place, lift the tank off the bowl and lay it down on the blanket on its back.

SUSIE'S HELPFUL HINTS

It's not only for aches and pains

Rubbing alcohol will help remove stains and mildew from the caulking around your tub.

Unscrew the locknut from the valve seat shaft and pull the valve seat into the tank. Then just replace the washer at the top of the shaft and the cone-shaped washer at its base.

Put it all back together, turn on the water, fill the tank and take your assistant to lunch on some of what you didn't pay the plumber.

YOU'VE GOTTA HAVE HOT— YOUR ELECTRIC WATER HEATER AND YOU

My friend Sheila, who lives in deepest Florida, called me to complain about her electric bill, knowing that I would lend a sympathetic ear. She told me that suddenly the little disk in her meter was spinning like a bingo wheel out of control, the electric company was getting rich and she couldn't figure out why.

SUSIE'S HELPFUL HINTS

A good temperature for hot water in the home is 120 degrees unless you have a dishwasher (The mechanical kind, not your husband or the kids). Then the thermostat should be set at 140 degrees.

Everything, everywhere had been checked and she was stumped. Being the kind of person I am I asked her if she had an electric water heater.

She said yes. I asked her if it had been flushed recently and if the thermostat was working properly. Sheila said it was brand new. Check your faucets for drips, I said. Not a one, she replied. Check the pipes I told her, there's a good chance you've got a leak. Sheila called me back a few days later and said I had mystical powers because her plumber had found a leaking pipe in the hot water line running from the heater—which was in the garage—to her house. The electric bill was sky high because hot water was draining away into the dirt under her Cadillac.

It's not that I'm a witch, it's just that I'd had a chillingly similar experience.

We live in a cold climate and nobody bothered to suggest we insulate the hot water pipes in the basement. The bottom line was that the electric company was getting rich while the water heater produced hot water that was cooling off as it moved up into the house. Top that off with a leaking hot water faucet in the bathroom and we were not only losing hundreds of gallons of hot water a year, we were paying through the nose.

Since Sheila lives in Florida, poor insulation was not the issue and a reasonable possibility was a leaking pipe. Case closed.

The point is your water heater needs attention just like your mother-in-law, only it's much easier to deal with.

HOT WATER HEATER

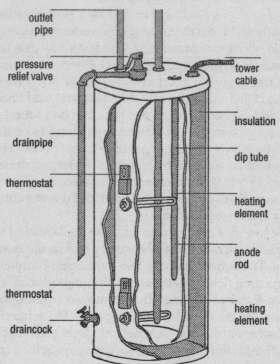

- outlet pipe
- pressure relief valve
- drainpipe
- thermostat
- thermostat
- draincock
- tower cable
- insulation
- dip tube
- heating element
- anode rod
- heating element

SOME COMMON WATER HEATER PROBLEMS

Sediment In The Tank No matter whether you use softened water or water laden with minerals, sediment will build up in the tank and interfere with the heating element's ability to do it's job. You can tell if there's a problem because you're burning up heating elements at a fast rate. If your water supply is hard the tank should be drained and flushed once a month—you'll notice the difference.

First turn off the water heater. Then turn the cold water supply to the water heater off and leave a hot water faucet running upstairs. Attach a length of garden hose to the drain cock and run it outdoors or to the nearest floor drain. Empty the tank. Leaving the drain cock open, turn on the cold water supply and run it until the water is clear. Close the drain cock and fill the tank with cold water until the faucet is running upstairs to signal that the tank is full. Turn the heater on and you're done.

Leaky Relief Valve The relief valve is located on top of the water heater and operates on the same principle as the valve on top of your pressure cooker. It prevents the heater from exploding if the thermostat fails and the water gets too hot. As it gets older the little

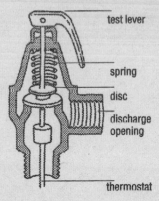

RELIEF VALVE

test lever

spring

disc

discharge opening

thermostat

spring weakens (just like us all) and it starts to release pressure for no reason. All you need to do is get a new one, turn off the heater and the water supply while you replace it. Remember to use your joint compound.

SUSIE'S HELPFUL HINTS

Don't sweat it

If you've got a problem with a sweaty toilet it's easy to fix. Sweat comes from the cold water in the tank causing warm humid air to condense on the surface. You can buy a ready-to-install liner for the tank or you can get a piece of 1/2 inch insulating foam rubber, some rubber cement or silicone glue and make it yourself.

Shut the water off at the shut-off valve on the water inlet pipe and drain the tank. Sponge it dry and cut a hole for the flush handle bracket. Fit it before you apply the glue to it and make sure the foam isn't in the way of any moving parts. Glue it in place and let it dry for twenty-four hours before you refill the tank.

IT'S SHOCKING BUT TRUE:
YOU'VE GOT THE POWER, USE IT

I was introduced to the fascinating world of electrical repairs by Elmo, our black dwarf rabbit. Elmo lives in a little cage in the kitchen, but he's also litter-trained, so we let him out every day to hop around the house. It's amusing to watch him chase the cats, but he also has an annoying habit of gnawing on things—or at least he did. One day Elmo was playing behind the couch in the living room when I heard a crackle and saw a puff of smoke rising up toward the window. Elmo scampered out, then collapsed, shaking like a leaf.

When I picked him up, I noticed that his whiskers had been singed right down to the fur. I pulled out the couch and saw why—he'd been chewing on the lamp wire. After I determined that Elmo was okay, I unplugged the lamp. As I was deciding what to do, my UPS man came to the door. I order a lot of stuff through the mail and he's become sort of a friend. I told him the story. He took a look at the cord, pulled out his knife, asked for some electrical tape and showed me how to splice the wires back together.

I couldn't believe how easy it was. Ladies, let me tell you this—wiring repairs are child's play compared with sewing. The manual dexterity and patience you need to thread a needle and hem a pair of pants far surpasses the skill required to rewire a lamp, install a dimmer switch, or hook up a ceiling fixture. As soon as I learned what to do, I discovered I was a lot better at it than my husband, and you can be, too.

Also, unlike plumbing, most things electrical involve clean indoor work.

ELECTRON RACEWAY

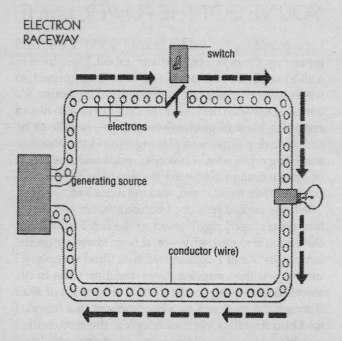

CIRCUITS, BREAKERS AND YOU:

UNDERSTANDING ELECTRICITY AND YOUR HOME'S ELECTRICAL SYSTEM

WHAT IS ELECTRICITY?

To most of us, electricity is what comes out of the box in the wall and makes our toaster work. It's mysterious, magical and totally beyond comprehension. In fact, electricity, and the electrical system in your house are pretty simple to understand and very logical in concept.

Your electrical system bears a striking resemblance to your plumbing system. There are differences, of course, and it doesn't mean that you can be up to your waders in water and change a light switch at the same time— unless you love surprises. But it helped me to think of all those little electrons flowing through wires as water flowing through pipes, and that switches and circuit breakers control its flow instead of faucets and valves.

IMPORTANT Minor electrical repairs are one thing, but if you get ambitious and decide to rewire the garage you'll need to contact the local authorities and get a permit. Although it's perfectly legal to work on the wiring in your home, you need to comply with safety codes and make sure the work is done properly. Believe me, this is a good thing and, while dealing with the local bureaucrats is never a pleasure, it's a lot worse than getting something done and finding out too late it was wrong. Improperly installed wiring can cause you headaches with the city, your insurance company and maybe cost you your life.

Electrons are like racehorses (see diagram on page 36). In order for them to do their job they need a place to run. My husband understands that part even if he won't fix the doorbell. In the electrical world, the racetrack is called a circuit. A circuit is simply a loop of wire that carries a flow of electrons (current) from the source to the outlet or whatever and back. That's why all cables have at least two wires in them—to create that all-important circle. Anyway, as long as the circuit is closed, all those little electrons just keep moving around in their little racetrack. But when the circuit is interrupted by any means at all, such as a wall switch, they stop and wait for the circuit to be closed again. I don't know what they do while they're waiting and I'm not sure I want to. But it really is that simple, when you turn a light switch on you complete the circuit and the light comes on. When you break the circuit the light goes off.

If the circuit is broken by anything other than the switch, the current won't flow and you have what we all know as a "short." That's what happened when Elmo chewed the wire.

VOLTS, AMPS, AND WATTS I used to think that volts, amps and watts were words invented by the electrical company to confuse the issue and make me think they were smarter than I was so they could raise my electric bill at random. That may still be true, but I feel better knowing what the words mean.

The flow of electrons through a circuit is measured in AMPERES just like the flow of water through your pipes is measured in gallons. (In case you're interested, one amp equals 6 1/4 billion electrons moving past a given point on a circuit in one second.) Also, just like water, the current of electricity is moved through the circuit by pressure. In the electrical system that pressure is called VOLTAGE. If you wanted to be an electrical engineer or a beancounter you could multiply the VOLTS times the amps and come up with the amount of current used or the WATTAGE. So, friends, a 100 watt bulb needs to draw 100 watts of current from the circuit in order to shed some light on the mess in Timmy's room.

Like I was saying, voltage is the pressure that delivers the amps to their destination. The higher the voltage, the faster those little electrons dance along. In a perfect world, that would be the end of it, but since we don't live in a perfect world there is a little matter called RESISTANCE. If you've ever run a really long extension cord to something and found it doesn't work to full capacity or a cord gets really hot, you've experienced resistance. George's resistance to taking out the garbage is another matter.

The longer the distance electrons have to travel, the more voltage or pressure they need because a certain percentage of the little guys are lost to resistance in the cable (or conductor). Over time, the people who think about these things came up with standardized voltage levels to provide necessary service. That's why most electrical services operate at 120 (household needs) or 240 volts (major appliances). Along the way they discovered that many applications such as doorbells, track lighting and the like, don't require as much voltage to operate efficiently and have designed LOW VOLTAGE SYSTEMS, usually 12 to 16 volts, to operate them. These systems operate off a transformer that "steps" the voltage down to the correct amount, saving power and therefore, money.

It's important to know a little about volts and amps for two reasons. One, they affect our electric bill and two, their designations affect how we approach repairs.

Watt Are We Talking About Here? Watts measure the power we draw from the electrical company to run our homes. All those spinning dials on the electric meter record the Watt Hours used and tell the meter reader the outrageous amount to charge us each month. The more we know about how we use electricity, the more money we can save.

Circuit breakers and fuses are measured in amps. They're designed to "trip" or blow if more current is demanded by the circuit than it is designed to supply. If you are constantly blowing fuses or tripping the breakers, it's a sign that you're overloading the system and it's time to find out why, because it can cause damage to appliances and fixtures and more importantly, start fires.

How It All Works Once again the faithful plumbing metaphor works like a charm in helping understand how the electrons make the journey from the power plant to your kitchen light.

Electricity is generated by huge turbines in far away places which are turned by a lot of different elements: water, fuels of all kinds and, interestingly enough to me anyway, air. Then it's sent, they actually say pumped, at very high voltage to distribution stations. The distribution stations do exactly that. They take the raw power, reduce it with transformers to more manageable voltages, and send it on to a vast network of successively

WATTS HAPPENING?

It's easy to figure out whether or not you've got enough watts available to do the job.

Make a list of the wattage that appears on each light fixture and appliance in the area served by the circuit breaker in question.

Multiply the amperage of the circuit breaker by the service voltage. For instance, **15 amps X 120 volts = 1800 watts** of potential use. If your wattage total exceeds that figure you need to upgrade the service, add a circuit or move the toaster oven to another room.

smaller systems that split it off to cities, rural areas and then to your home.

If your service is above ground, you can see the pole in the backyard with the little box on it (It's another transformer, which has a tendency in rural areas to fry curious squirrels and black out your entire house—at least that's what happens to me.) and you can see the wires running to the side of your house. If your home is older, the service is most likely to be 30 amps of power at 120 volts. This has proven to be inadequate in the modern age, what with Nintendo and air conditioners, etc. and most modern homes are routinely provided with services of 60 to 200 amps at 120/240 volts.

If you don't see the electric pole, your service runs underground.

The feed from the electric pole connects to an electric meter which is provided by the utility company. It records the amount of watts that flow into your home and is the basis of your electric bill. The meter is tagged and sealed by the utility to prevent those of you with a more entrepreneurial spirit from tampering with it.

From the meter, big wires run into your house and connect to the main service panel. You can guess how much power you're getting by looking at the number of wires. If you see two, one black and one white, your service is probably 30amp/120volt. Two blacks and one white usually indicates 60+amp/120-240 volts.

Just like you need to know the place where the main water shutoffs hide, you should know where the main electrical service panel is, in case you ever need to turn off all the power, to replace a fuse, or fix something for instance.

The main service panel, a boring gray in color, is yet another distribution center. In an older house it will probably contain only the main disconnect and the

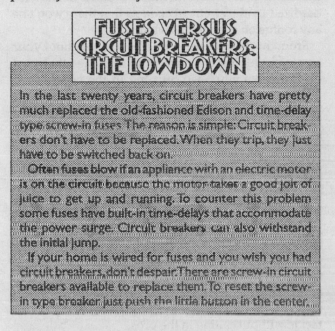

FUSES VERSUS CIRCUIT BREAKERS: THE LOWDOWN

In the last twenty years, circuit breakers have pretty much replaced the old-fashioned Edison and time-delay type screw-in fuses. The reason is simple: Circuit breakers don't have to be replaced. When they trip, they just have to be switched back on.

Often fuses blow if an appliance with an electric motor is on the circuit because the motor takes a good jolt of juice to get up and running. To counter this problem some fuses have built-in time-delays that accommodate the power surge. Circuit breakers can also withstand the initial jump.

If your home is wired for fuses and you wish you had circuit breakers, don't despair. There are screw-in circuit breakers available to replace them. To reset the screw-in type breaker just push the little button in the center.

circuit breakers or fuses will appear in subpanels stocked with fuses or circuit breakers at various locations around the house.

More recent panels will contain the main disconnect as well as a row of circuit breakers. These, in turn, split the service throughout your home. With 30/120 you will see one black wire which is called the "hot" wire, a white wire which is called the "neutral" wire and a green which is called the "ground." The green wire attaches to a grounding rod or metal plumbing pipes. It's there to defuse any excess electricity off into the ground where it can't hurt anybody. These colors are the same everywhere because they've been standardized by the electrical code so that there won't be any confusion over what's what.

From the main panel, wires flow throughout your house supplying the current to switches that turn on the lights you keep burning in the window, so

---

SUSIE'S HELPFUL HINTS

Confused thinking

Don't think that you are solving the problem by putting a 20 amp fuse or breaker in a circuit designed to carry 15 amps. While it may seem to work fine, what's really happening is the circuit is overloading and could eventually cause a fire. If you need more power, upgrade the service.

George and the kids can find their way home from soccer practice at night.

At this point there are lots of projects that you can tackle without calling in the pros.

And just like with plumbing, you have to shut it off to work on it.

NO SUDDEN JOLTS:

TURNING THE POWER OFF AND PUTTING SAFETY FIRST WHEN WORKING WITH ELECTRICITY

Some of us think, for reasons that are totally beyond me, that it's hysterical when Mo sticks Curley's finger in the light socket and he dances around the room like an idiot while his hair smokes and gets frizzy. It's guaranteed to make my kids howl with glee and try to poke each other's eyes out. But, if you've ever been jolted by a shot of electricity, you know that, no matter how funny it might seem on television, it isn't a joke. Now, I'm not trying to scare you away from jobs you can easily do yourself, but like my grandfather said, "you gotta respect it or it'll bite you."

Like solving any other home repair problem, careful preparation and knowing what the potential hazards are takes the fear away and can really save you money. Carelessness makes electricity dangerous and yet the steps you can take to protect yourself when doing electrical repairs are very logical and simple. It's just a matter of common sense—don't do something you haven't thought through, and fully understand. Maybe I should have followed that advice before I subscribed to all those magazines to try to win a million dollars.

SAFETY FIRST: COMMON ELECTRICAL SENSE

Always shut down the power to the circuit you're going to work on at the main service panel. Label each circuit breaker clearly so you know exactly what you're switching on and off.

No matter how convenient it seems, don't run extension cords under carpets or rugs. If the cord frays you've got trouble.

Whether you're using your hairdryer or fixing a switch, don't touch radiators or faucets at the same time. Your electrical system is probably grounded to the plumbing system and if something's wrong you could be in for a shock.

Don't let Timmy take the radio into the bathtub and don't do it yourself either.

When you use an adapter to make a three-prong plug fit into a two-prong receptacle, make sure you take the little green grounding wire and hook it to the screw in the receptacle plate.

Don't replace a fuse with another one of higher amperage. There's a reason why the smaller fuse is blowing.

When you remove a plug from the wall, don't pull it out by the cord. The connections will loosen, overheat and become a fire hazard.

Unplug anything before you work on it.

Use your circuit tester to double check that a circuit is off before you work on it.

Wear your rubber boots if you're working on a damp floor.

PART THREE

TOOLS OF THE TRADE:

EVERYTHING YOU NEED FOR SIMPLE ELECTRICAL REPAIRS

WHAT'S IN THE BOX?

One of the things that will become clearer the farther you get down the road to Home Repair Heaven is that many of the tools you need to do various jobs also do lots of others. As I said when we were talking about plumbing, buy the tools you need for various repairs and keep them organized and orderly in a convenient location—so you'll know exactly where to find them—and, so once you've found them,

---

HERE'S WHAT I CARRY IN MINE

- ❑ circuit tester
- ❑ claw hammer
- ❑ continuity tester
- ❑ diagonal wire cutters
- ❑ electrician's pliers

- ❑ electrician's tape
- ❑ flashlight
- ❑ mat knife
- ❑ needlenose pliers
- ❑ power drill and bits

- ❑ rubber boots
- ❑ slotted screwdrivers
- ❑ terminal screwdrivers
- ❑ wire nuts
- ❑ wire strippers
- ❑ wood chisel

everything you need is there, whether it's for an emergency or a more leisurely project.

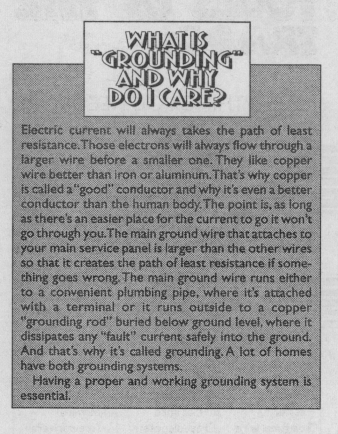

WHAT IS "GROUNDING" AND WHY DO I CARE?

Electric current will always takes the path of least resistance. Those electrons will always flow through a larger wire before a smaller one. They like copper wire better than iron or aluminum. That's why copper is called a "good" conductor and why it's even a better conductor than the human body. The point is, as long as there's an easier place for the current to go it won't go through you. The main ground wire that attaches to your main service panel is larger than the other wires so that it creates the path of least resistance if something goes wrong. The main ground wire runs either to a convenient plumbing pipe, where it's attached with a terminal or it runs outside to a copper "grounding rod" buried below ground level, where it dissipates any "fault" current safely into the ground. And that's why it's called grounding. A lot of homes have both grounding systems.

Having a proper and working grounding system is essential.

PART FOUR

I CAN FIX THAT—

KEEPING A LIGHT BURNING IN THE WINDOW

MAKING A CIRCUIT MAP OF YOUR HOME If you haven't done this already, I suggest it should be the very first thing you do before becoming your own electrician. It's amazing to me how many people don't even bother to look inside their circuit breaker box until they need something from it, as in which breaker controls the hot tub that's out of action on the patio or the washing machine that's bucking like a bronco in the basement. If pressed, most people will say that they meant to label everything but just never got around to it. Well, all that does is heighten the electrical mystery and make it harder to get things done.

Drawing a simple map of your home showing where all the outlets and appliances live, and what circuits they're hooked up to, will make it a lot easier to trace the source of a problem when something goes wrong. Number each outlet or appliance on the map. Then grab one of your kids and go to work. Plug a lamp or a radio into each outlet and turn all the switches on.

Take your station at the breaker panel and have your children stand at the ready. Then, one by one, start switching off the breakers. Let Timmy yell back to you (but remind him that it's only OK to shout when your're working) back to you which outlets went out with which circuit breaker, note the circuit breaker number in the appropriate place on the map and put the outlet information on a label next to its breaker. Continue until all the breakers are accounted for and put the map in a plastic sleeve or envelope, hang it up next to the panel and congratulate yourself on a job well done.

Now we're ready to shed a little light on some simple projects that'll make you the envy of the electrician's union.

PLUGS AND CORDS There are any number of reasons why you might want to put a different plug on an appliance or make up an extension cord. Maybe the prongs have been bent or broken, the casing has cracked, there's a short inside, you need to ground the outlet, or you're tired of paying for ready-mades and want to make up some extension cords yourself.

Putting a new plug on the end of a piece of wire is a piece of cake. In fact, it's so simple that it's a great way to get acquainted with electrical hardware and try out your skills with some of the tools. You get to play with clippers, wire cutters, cable strippers, and screwdrivers. I know you'll say that everybody knows how to use a screwdriver but, believe me, some of the screws you run into doing electrical work are tiny little fellows and it takes some practice to manage them.

Plugs come in literally hundreds of shapes and sizes, from simple snap-ons for regular Zip cord, to the three-prong "twist-lock" monsters used for major appliances and other big things. But no matter how big or small they all work in the same way—whether it's two little prongs of a screwless "clip on" plug pressing through the insulation and making contact with the wire or giant screw terminals that the wire wraps around and then is tightened into place.

The basic rules of Fix-It apply:

* Take a look at what you're doing before you start.
* Get the right tools in place.
* Remember how you took it apart so you can put it together the same way.
* Buy an exact replacement.
* Go to work.

It's essential that you use wire cable that's up to the job you've intended it for. You'll be very disappointed if you try to run the electric lawnmower on regular household Zip cord. As a matter of fact, next time you're in the hardware store look at the rolls of electrical cable. You'll see that they come in several thicknesses or "gauges" and are rated in amps. The higher the rating the more current the cable can handle. The counter people can help you get the right size or "gauge" of wire for the job.

There are two options for removing a damaged plug from a piece of cable. One: you can take it apart to learn how to put it back together or Two: you can do it the fun way (once you understand how it works)—take your wire clippers and just snip the cable. It's fast, and a great way to deal with a lot of life's little frustrations. If George and the kids ship me off to the funny farm, all I want is a room full of wire cable, some plugs and my electrical kit. Nobody's going to get hurt and the world will have all the extension cords it can handle.

Anyway, there isn't much to say about snap-on plugs—they snap on. The biggest problem is making sure you get the right size plug for the wire you're using. Round wire plugs, on the other hand, require a little more effort but in the end you have a better and sturdier product. (Remember, cords undergo a lot of wear and tear.)

First, strip the rubber sheathing back from the end of the cable about 2 inches. Use a cable stripper or a mat knife. Just be careful not to cut the insulation around the wires inside the cable. Underneath the rubber casing there might be a layer of fiber. Cut that away as well to expose the wires (they're wrapped in colored insulation). Use your cable strippers to remove about 3/4 of an inch of the insulation to expose the copper wire. You'll notice the wire is made of tiny strands wrapped together. Twist them clockwise until tight. Run the cable through the plug and tie what's called an *"Underwriter's Knot"* before you screw the wire to the terminals. (The knot makes sure there's no stress on the connections when the cord is inevitably yanked around.) If you're dealing with a two-wire plug, you'll see two terminals—one is brass, and the other, silver. The black or "hot" wire goes to the brass and the white "neutral" goes to the silver. If the cable is grounded you'll attach the green "ground" wire to the green terminal. Sometimes with grounded cable you'll find that there isn't room to knot all three so just do the black and white.

BECOMING AN ELECTRICAL GUMSHOE: FINDING AND FIXING SHORTS AND OVERLOADS

There I was, standing at the counter folding the laundry and watching to make sure the supper potatoes didn't boil over, when the lights went off for the second time that afternoon and I was left in semi-darkness with George's underwear in my hands and the lid rattling on the stove. The kids didn't move from the TV, but at least they asked Mommy what happened. Of course, I couldn't remember where I'd put the flashlight and so, after stumbling to the breaker box and searching for the right switch, I knew I had to do something. So, I put on my fedora hat, cinched up my trenchcoat and became a private detective, seeking the source of the darkness in my kitchen.

If you're not certain whether the circuit is breaking because of a short or an overload, you really do become a detective, using logic and your powers of deduction to expose the culprits. Finding the source of an electrical problem takes patience and the willingness to eliminate the suspects one by one in a logical order. Sometimes you get lucky, and the problem presents itself right away, but don't count on it. One of the ancient laws is that you will always find what you're seeking in the last place you look. And remember, your electrician has to do exactly the same thing, but he's charging you money while he does it.

Finding Out What's Wrong If a fuse or breaker blows or trips repeatedly, the next time you replace it, see how long it takes to blow again. If the thing pops instantly there's a good chance you've got a short, usually in an appliance or lamp connection, or an extension cord, or in the wiring of a lamp, or less likely, a ceiling fixture. Look for obvious damage like a frayed cord or a plug that's loose or very warm to the touch. If it's not the cords or connections then the short's hidden deeper in the system. On the other hand, if the breaker or fuse takes time to fry, you've got an overload and the immediate solution is to lighten the electrical demand.

Do The Math (See: WATTS HAPPENING? page 41) Figure out whether there's too much wattage for the circuit to handle. Then unplug things until the problem stops and think about adding more circuits. However, if the problem doesn't go away, you've got a short, or what some electricians call *Mr. Sparky*. Unplug everything in the section controlled by the fuse or breaker and turn off all switches, go to your trusty tool box and get your continuity and circuit testers and a slotted screwdriver.

Searching Out Mr. Sparky Turn on the breaker or insert a new fuse. If the fuse blows, loosen it so you're sure it's not making contact or if the breaker trips,

SUSIE'S HELPFUL HINTS

Wrap the cable around the terminal in a clockwise direction. When you screw it down the cable will be drawn tightly into the terminal for a solid connection.

turn it off and shut the panel door. The reason for leaving the blown fuse loose in its receptacle is that you don't want someone to stick a finger in the empty socket. Remember, the main power is still on and the socket is live. If you have people in the house, it won't hurt to put a sign on the panel box saying something pithy like "George, don't touch this on pain of death."

It's time to check the outlets and switches for damage.

To make sure the current is really down, turn the switches on and off. Check the receptacles by inserting the tips of the circuit tester in the slots of the outlet. If the little light at the top doesn't go on, it's safe to begin working. For the switches you'll have to remove the cover plate, take the tester and touch one of the probes to a terminal screw and one to the junction box. Do the same with the other screw. If the light doesn't come on you can forge ahead.

Remove the cover plates from each outlet and switch and look for damage, like broken receptacles or loose wires. Take a small slotted screwdriver, remove the screws that hold the switch or receptacle in place and gently pull the unit out of its junction box. In most cases you'll see two stiff copper wires, one sheathed in black and one in white. Remember that the black one is called the "hot" wire and the white is called the "neutral." Because you've tested them, however, you know they're dead and the only shock you'll get is if you can't remember where you put the little screws when you want to put it all back together.

Take your screwdriver and check the screws that hold the terminal wires in place to see if any have loosened and tighten them down. It seems as if something that looks as solid and permanent as a screw should just stay in place once it's tightened down, but vibration over an extended period of time or the patron saint of the electrician's union can cause screws to loosen. Sometimes it's that simple.

**Over Here Dr. Watson,
I Think I've Found Something** If you find something obvious like a terminal wire that's come totally off the switch or receptacle, screw it back into place. After you've checked all the receptacles and switches put them back in their boxes. Turn the switches to the off position. (You can leave the cover plates off just in case you have to go back in.) If a wall switch controls an outlet, plug something into the outlet.

Turn on the power at the box, flip the switches one by one and see what happens. If you flip a switch and the circuit blows you've nailed it. The problem is the switch or the fixture or outlet it controls. The first thing to do is test the switch itself. Turn off the power and remove the switch from the box and unscrew the wires. Take your continuity tester and clip the little alligator clip to one of the terminal screws, touch the tip of the tester probe to the other screw. If the little light goes on the switch is good. Put it back together and back in the box.

Eureka! Now you know it's either the appliance or the ceiling fixture—we'll get to ceiling fixtures later—that the switch runs, the outlet (if the switch controls one), or whatever's plugged into the outlet. Remove the outlet and give it the old continuity test, as with the switch. If the light goes on the outlet is good and can be returned to its place. Now you know it's in the fixture or appliance and you can look for damage there after you put the system back together.

If, after all this, the problem won't go away, you've got to call in the pros, but at least you know that you've done everything possible to protect your checking account.

RE-SHEDDING THE LIGHT Like anything else, the best electrical hardware can go bad and need to be

A SHORT-CIRCUIT AND A GROUND FAULT—WHAT'S THE DIFFERENCE?

In truth, not much. They're both referred to as "shorts" but the difference is important.

A short circuit usually occurs when a cord frays or a plug is damaged. As the insulation wears thin, the hot wire and the neutral will come into contact with one another and the circuit is "shortcutted" through the connection. This creates a surge of electrons and enough heat to make the flash you've probably seen when a plug or cord goes. Once the point of contact is burned away, the short is over but you can see the black marks where it occurred and you know exactly what to fix.

A ground fault, on the other hand, happens when a wire comes loose from a terminal inside a switch or junction box. The wire makes contact with the metal box and the current (seeking the path of least resistance, as always) flows through the box back down to the main ground wire where most of it dissipates into the ground. However, it's possible that not all the current will go away so the box remains "hot", and if you touch it you will become the path of least resistance or the ground for that circuit. That's generally what happens when people are accidentally electrocuted in their homes—unless they insist on doing stupid things like setting the hairdryer in the damp sink while they fix their hair or balancing the radio on the edge of the bathtub.

replaced. The important thing is to replace it with the
right one and do the job correctly. Once again logic
and preparation are the keys. Before you remove the

SUSIE'S HELPFUL HINT

Check to make sure that all fuses are tightly screwed
into their sockets. Loose fuses will sometimes blow.

unit look at how it was installed and remember it.
When I was getting started I liked to draw a little picture of where everything went, just so I wouldn't
panic when it was time to put it all back together.
Also, get a dish or cup or something to hold any loose
screws so you don't have to search for them later.

Unless you're replacing something to upgrade it in
some manner—like adding a timer switch to what
used to be just a simple double outlet —take the critter you want to replace to the hardware store and get
one just like it. The units are engraved with information such as its ratings for amps and volts, the proper
kind of wire to hook it up with, and the tester's stamp
of approval. All that information is there for a reason—the wrong unit can cause serious problems.

INSTALLING RECEPTACLES There are two basic
types of receptacles, side-wired, which have screw terminals on the side, and back-wired, which use "push-
in" terminals instead of screws. It's always best to put in
what you took out because you know it will fit in the
junction box.

Do the **Shut Off The Power** thing, test to make sure the circuit is dead, and remove the faulty receptacle by unscrewing the terminal screws and removing the wires. Receptacles are designated by where they appear in the electrical run. The "end-of-the-run" receptacles (which are also at the beginning of the run) will have only one HOT wire and one NEUTRAL whereas the MIDDLE-OF-THE-RUN receptacle will have two HOTS, one incoming and the

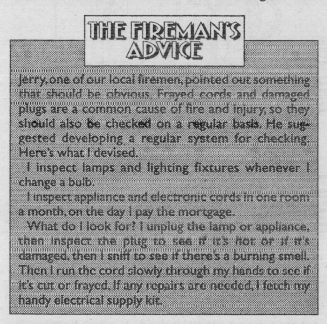

THE FIREMAN'S ADVICE

Jerry, one of our local firemen, pointed out something that should be obvious. Frayed cords and damaged plugs are a common cause of fire and injury, so they should also be checked on a regular basis. He suggested developing a regular system for checking. Here's what I devised.

I inspect lamps and lighting fixtures whenever I change a bulb.

I inspect appliance and electronic cords in one room a month, on the day I pay the mortgage.

What do I look for? I unplug the lamp or appliance, then inspect the plug to see if it's hot or if it's damaged, then I sniff to see if there's a burning smell. Then I run the cord slowly through my hands to see if it's cut or frayed. If any repairs are needed, I fetch my handy electrical supply kit.

other outgoing. The same with the NEUTRALS. Just hook them up like you found them.

Also don't be dismayed by double (four-receptacle)

DUPLEX
RECEPTACLE

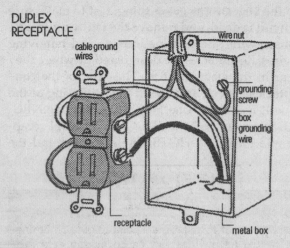

outlets. There are a few more wires, but the process is the same. Just make a good map before you remove anything.

You'll note that the wire in a junction box is solid instead of braided like zip cord and somebody twisted a hook at the end to grab the screw. Clip off the old hook with your wire cutters, take your mat knife or a cable stripper and remove about 3/4 of an inch of the insulation. Make a new hook by bending it with your needlenose pliers and set it around the terminal screw so that the direction of the hook is going clockwise. This will pull the hook tightly into the screw when you tighten it. You'll know if you've got the wire on the wrong side because turning the screw will push the wire off the terminal. The black or HOT wire goes to the brass screw and the white NEUTRAL goes to the silver one. The green GROUND wire, if there is one, attaches to a little screw at the base of the receptacle.

After making sure everything's tight, set the new unit back in the box and screw it into place. Put the cover back on, power it up and let the juice flow.

INSTALLING AND REPLACING SWITCHES The process for changing a light switch is essentially the same as changing a receptacle. Remember how you took it apart, get the correct replacement and go to work. Sometimes the trickiest part of the whole thing is getting all the wires and the switch stuffed back in the box, but a little patience will win the day. Remember, somebody got it in there the first time so you can, too.

There are four basic types of switches:

The Single Pole Switch is the most common. It simply opens or closes a single circuit when you toggle it up or down. It has On and Off engraved on the switch handle. Poles, by the way, simply designate the number of brass terminals available to connect "hot" wires.

The Double Pole Switch has two "hot" connections and is used to handle 240 volt outlets and major appliances. Like the single pole, it has On and Off designations.

The Three-Way Switch is used to give you the ability to control a light from two different locations.

The Four-Way Switch is used to control an appliance or lighting system from three or more locations.

REWIRING LAMPS There's no reason to toss Grandma's favorite lamp just because every time you switch it on the house goes dark. Rewiring a lamp is easy and a great way to spend a cold winter afternoon. As a matter of fact, once you know the basics of lamp repair, you can purchase the pieces and make your own, using any number of interesting items for bases.

Unplug the lamp, of course, and remove the shade. The horseshoe-like piece that holds the shade is called the harp and simply snaps out of the retaining sleeves

SWITCHING SWITCHES

The beauty of knowing how to replace a light switch is that it gives you the option of exchanging your existing switches with specialty jobs that can be real problem solvers. For instance, you can add a DIMMER SWITCH to the dining room to make the room more romantic and save energy at the same time. There are LOCKING SWITCHES that require a key to open and therefore guarantee that things like stereos and power tools can be safe from prying little hands. You can put a LIGHTED SWITCH in the basement or garage so you can see what you're aiming for. Or how about a TIME-DELAY SWITCH that allows you to get from one place to another before the light goes out. Then there's a TIMER SWITCH with a clock that will turn the lights on and off at specified time to keep the thieves at bay while you're away from home. There's even a PILOT SWITCH that has a light to remind you that you left the porch light on after sending the cat out into the night. And, last but not least, a MOTION DETECTOR SWITCH will actually turn a light off automatically when you leave the room.

All you have to do is make sure that your junction box is big enough to hold the replacement and you're in business. Often you can simply replace the old box with a deeper one to give yourself more room.

when you squeeze it. On the lamp socket you'll find the word PRESS. Do that and the socket will pop out so you can pull out the metal shell and its insulating sleeve. This will reveal the lamp switch itself.

Now go to the bottom of the lamp. Remove the base cover (usually felt) carefully, so you can put it back later. Take your wire cutters and snip the old cable about a foot from the base of the lamp. Strip an inch or so of insulation from the old cord and from the cord you're going to replace it with. Twist the ends of old and new together and wrap them with a piece of electrician's tape.

Next pull the new cord into the lamp base and up through the hole at the top. Snip off the old cord and strip 3/4 of an inch of insulation off the new one. If you're not replacing the switch and socket, remove the old wire and attach the new one to the terminals.

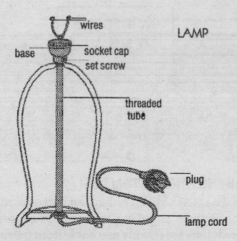

LAMP

wires

base — socket cap
set screw

threaded tube

plug

lamp cord

A Common Mistake Now—and this is the part even the pros sometimes forget in the heat of battle—before you hook the wire to the terminals, thread the wire through the socket base. Otherwise you'll have to remove the wire again to assemble the socket.

SUSIE'S HELPFUL HINTS

Buy only electrical parts (like switches and plugs) that have the Underwriter's Laboratory (UL) stamp of approval. The stamp means that they've been tested and found safe to use in the home.

Once the wires are firmly in place, reassemble the socket and set it back on the lamp base. Knot the cord inside the lamp near the base to reduce stress on the connections, replace the felt, put on a new plug, flick it on and test to make sure the lamp works by spending the rest of the afternoon reading a mystery.

A LITTLE PEP TALK

I know this all sounds complicated but if you stick with it, sooner or later the little light will pop on in your head and suddenly you'll wonder why it all seemed so difficult. When that happens you've crossed a major bridge and you're well on your way to becoming a veteran Fixer-Upper.

REPAIRING AND INSTALLING
LIGHTING FIXTURES
The hardest part of working on lighting fixtures is getting to them. Of course, wall-mounted units are usually reachable from the floor, but

for ceiling units you need a ladder and that may take some getting used to. Some people are very comfortable with heights, others learn to become comfortable (like me) and the rest just can't deal with it. You should never, and I repeat never, work on a ladder if you aren't

SUSIE'S HELPFUL HINTS

Sometimes electricians will run a strip of electrical tape around the terminals to help keep the screws from coming loose.

100% confident and secure, it isn't worth it. A lighting fixture that looks like a piece of cake on the ground can be a real bear when you're standing several feet in the air, trying to balance the fixture, hold a screwdriver and keep track of all the little pieces you need to put it together. When the job is done, it's very satisfying and exciting to look up there and say I did that, but only if you're not wearing a cast at the time. If you do feel comfortable working in the air, however, replacing and repairing lighting fixtures can save you money.

As always, disconnect the power that feeds the fixture circuit and test to be sure it's down before you begin.

SUSIE'S HELPFUL HINTS

Make sure you leave enough "extension" on the cord to reach your intended outlet.

Making A Plan You may have to study the problem for a little while to see how the old fixture comes apart. Usually, the globe is secured by little nuts or tension springs or any number of other devices. It may take a while, but eventually you'll figure it out.

Remove the globe and the light bulbs. From this point on, the means of attaching the new one should be pretty clear, and the new fixture should come with instructions plus all the hardware you'll need.

The junction box is mounted flush into the ceiling and when you remove the old base you'll see the way the wires are connected. If you think you can't remember what it looks like later, do a diagram. At any rate, study it until you're sure how everything goes together.

Note that the wires are connected by little plastic caps called wire nuts. These little inventions have pretty much replaced electrician's tape for these kinds of connections and will make your life much easier. To connect the fixture wires to the wires in the junction box, twist them together and screw the wire nut down over them. It's easy and very secure—just make sure that the nuts are the correct size for the wire.

The fixture will attach to the junction box in one of two ways. Either from what is called a stud (a threaded rod that comes down through the center of the ceiling box) or a strap (a metal bar that spans the junction box and screws into the holes at the ends of the box.) The one you need should be provided with the new fixture. If not, a trip to the hardware store will get you what you want.

From this point on, it's a matter of feeding the wires down through the center hole of the strap, or if you're hanging the fixture from a stud through a little device called a "hickey" (don't you love it?). Sometimes a heavy fixture will have both.

IMPORTANT Don't ever bite off more than you can chew. If you're hanging a heavy chandelier in the dining room or a ceiling fan in the bedroom you're probably going to need help. Or maybe you'll want to consider a professional.

The key is to prepare in advance and have a plan. Work carefully and slowly and you'll enjoy the results.

REPAIRING AND INSTALLING DOORBELLS AND CHIMES

As the drill sergeant at Fix-It boot camp might have yelled at the new recruits, "This is your doorbell. It has four basic parts. Make them your friends." But, anyway, your doorbell does have four basic parts and repairing or replacing it is a good introduction to the world of low-voltage. The parts are: a pushbutton switch, a signal unit, all the wiring, and a transformer to "step down" the house 120V service to 12 or 16 volts.

The transformer attaches to a junction box with bolts and the circuit runs to the switch, back through the bell or chime to the transformer where it completes itself.

If the bell isn't working, check the fuse or breaker. Remember: always try the simple things first.

Safety First Some people will tell you that because it takes so little current to run a low-voltage system, you don't really have to shut down the circuit to work

on it and that's sort of true but—what if the problem
is in the transformer? That's a big 120V comin' at you
full steam if you're wrong and it's not worth the risk,
so test it first. Take your trusty voltage tester and see
what's what. If your reading shows 120V instead of
12 or 16, the problem is the transformer. Replace it
and you're done. If the transformer is working properly, you can work on the system "live." Susie says,
"Follow the rules and you won't get hurt."

One Step At A Time Let's continue. If the
transformer seems OK, then the problem is
somewhere else. Once again logic will be our friend.
Assuming the voltage is correct, start with the push
button itself. Take off the plate and examine for loose
connections or broken wires. If everything looks
good, place your circuit tester probes on the
terminals. If the lamp lights, we know the switch
works and the transformer is probably going bad.

If the lamp doesn't light, take an insulated screwdriver (one with a rubber handle) and place the blade
across the terminals. If the bell rings then the button is

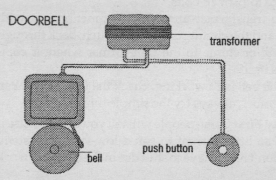

DOORBELL

transformer

bell

push button

corroded or broken. Remove it and use fine sandpaper to clean out the terminals and contacts. Hook it up again and if it still doesn't work replace it.

If it still doesn't work, check the wiring again both at the transformer and the switch. Sometimes remaking the connections will do the trick.

If everything seems to be working, forge your way back to the transformer and use a 12 volt circuit tester. If it doesn't light up, turn off the power and replace the

THE COLD HARD FACTS

I'm not obsessed about sealing up my house to keep in the heat (I've got a neighbor who is such a fanatic, you have to enter a pressure chamber to get in and out of the house). But I also don't like the idea of heating the outdoors when I'm paying for it. So when I learned how much heat escapes through electrical outlets and wall plates on outside walls, I decided to do something about it.

No matter how careful the contractor was when he installed the insulation, he undoubtedly left gaps and sometimes gaping holes around the wire runs and junction boxes. The result is that cold air has easy access to the house through the outlets.

On a cold windy night, light a candle and move around the house, holding it near the outlets (explain what you're doing to George and the kids so they don't call for the men in white suits). If the flame flickers, you've got a case of the drafts.

The good news is, the solution is cheap and easy. Insulating foam gaskets cut to fit inside the receptacle come packaged in quantity. To install one all you have to do is remove the cover plate and fit it in place.

Believe me it's worth it.

transformer. If it does light, the problem is in the bell unit. Get a duplicate and replace it.

The next time the doorbell rings, it won't be the mailman with a bill from your electrician.

If you're a typical mother like me, you're paranoid about your children's safety. You don't start the car until seat belts are fastened, you keep the cleaning supplies at near ceiling height, and you don't let your child wander away at the mall without an armed escort. My mania about safety is one reason I was doubly embarrassed one day when I answered the door and found two of our local firemen standing on the stoop. To add to my humiliation, one of them, Jerry, was married to Sue, who used to babysit for my children, and had to endure the 45-minute safety and emergency lecture I delivered every time I prepared to walk out the door.

Anyway, Jerry and his friend were going house to house to check smoke detectors. Sure enough, they found three dead batteries in our four detectors. Everyone looked at me as if I'd just handed a loaded revolver to my toddler, then my four-year old said, "Mommy, do you want us to burn to death?"

Fortunately, Jerry took pity on me and explained that our house was the rule rather than the exception. He gave me a simple system to keep the detectors working: change the batteries in all smoke detectors every six months on the same night you turn the clocks ahead or back. Since the look from my children is burned into my brain, I do it religiously.

SECTION THREE:

I CAN FIX THAT— NAILED

WHERE THERE'S A WALL, THERE'S A WAY

I'm one of the few people in the world who knows how Salman Rushdie feels, because I spent a few weeks as a despised and hunted outcast after an incident that will always been known in our family annals as:

THE DAY THE BOOKSHELF COLLAPSED

This debacle occurred about forty-five minutes after I'd completed one of my very first home improvement jobs—mounting a two-foot-long shelf next to the stove to hold my cookbooks. Sure, the cookbooks had been cozy and comfortable packed in a cardboard box in the rear of my upstairs closet, but I'd burned more meals than I could count when I had to run upstairs and rummage through that mini-junkpile to figure out why the beef stew tasted more like slightly salty water. So one day when I was in the hardware store anyway, I bought a shelf board and two brackets. I expected the project to take half the day, but I just fastened the brackets to the wall with the screws that came in the package and, voilà, there was my shelf! I was so proud that I invited Cindy Rawson over for a glass of wine.

For years Cindy had been the neighborhood organizer whose home looked like a *House Beautiful* cover. Not having a child had been the only flaw in her otherwise perfect life, but after a fortune in doctor's fees, she finally gave birth to a darling little girl, whom she brought over in her stroller. I was just opening the bottle when I heard a deafening crash. The shelf had given way, strewing hardcover books all over the place. Somehow, the baby escaped unscathed, but she was so scared that she let out an awful shriek. Cindy gave me a look that would have turned Hercules into stone, then dashed out to tell everyone in the neighborhood that I had deliberately tried to kill her baby.

SUSIE'S HELPFUL HINTS

Watch the shows

Home improvement shows are all over the cable networks and they're great to watch, especially once you've begun to grasp the basics. The more knowledge you have, the more they can help you. Also you'll begin to see that no matter how big the project the process is the same.

What I'd really done was stupid rather than criminal. I had always thought the walls of my house were made of wood, just like the doors and window sills. That day, I learned that they were made of something called wallboard, which crumbles into dust if you whack it with a hammer. Screws don't bite into it, they just shred it.

Ted at the hardware store managed to suppress his laugh when I told him the story. And he did help solve the problem. But no matter how nice he was, going into a large hardware store as a fix-it beginner was still a daunting exercise. Seeing row after row of objects that seemed beyond explanation, hanging from displays that reached to the ceiling, was bad enough. But listening to confident people chat knowingly about why the semi-torkel was far superior to the full one, while holding a screaming child and trying to figure out the difference between a carriage bolt and a lag bolt, is a guaranteed headache.

Even worse than trying to figure out the impossible by myself was having to go the counter and ask the man sheepishly for "that little round thing, you know, it's round...but it's got these funny edges." Then I would stare at the floor and have to confess, "no, I didn't bring it with me." As I walked to my car I was sure that everyone in the store was doubled over in hysterical laughter at Susie's expense.

Now, however, after gaining some experience and confidence and learning how to ask questions, I walk into hardware stores like Timmy walks into Disneyland—full of joy and wonder. The wizards of fix-it have come up with some of the most fascinating things to solve problems and make my life easier.

Of all the variety of home improvement projects and repairs, I think the ones involving carpentry are my favorites. There's nothing like the smell of freshly cut wood or the satisfaction of making, fixing or hanging something that you and your family touch and see every day. It's hard to describe, but the feeling of putting something together and seeing it work is a great one—and one we should all experience before they come to wheel us away.

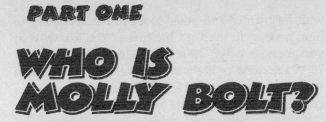

PART ONE

WHO IS MOLLY BOLT?

A GUIDE TO ALL THE TOOLS, MATERIALS AND HARDWARE YOU'LL NEED TO KEEP YOUR HOME SHIP-SHAPE

THE FIRST ONE'S IMPORTANT

The first real tool in my collection came to me when I wasn't even considering doing home improvement work on my own. We had just moved into the house and a grumpy contractor named Joe was taking forever to finish renovating the kitchen. I was hovering around thinking I was somehow speeding up the task when, in fact, I was only irritating him. One day I was watching him tear down a wall when the lunch break came. He went outside to eat and I stood looking at the chaos in my kitchen, wondering if he was ever going to get done. I was pushing absently on an exposed stud when something clattered to the ground at my feet. Just as I was picking it up, the contractor walked back into the kitchen and said he didn't like people touching his tools.

After telling him defensively that it fell out of the

wall, he grunted and asked to see it. When I gave it to him, his eyes lit up like Christmas. "You know what you got here, lady?" he asked. "This here is a Stanley 750." I nodded politely and he went on to tell me it was only manufactured from 1930 to 1969 and was a classic, "like a '52 Corvette or something."

It was a pretty object, with its beveled blade and hickory handle, and though he offered to buy it from me and was disappointed when I decided to keep it, he sharpened it up and showed me some chisel basics. Several more years passed before I actually decided to take up projects and home repair, but I think the seed was planted the day I found what some unlucky carpenter lost so long ago. Now I wouldn't part with my Stanley 750 for anything. As Harvey the ancient woodworker told me years later, "wood is your friend, but good tools are your family."

The world of tools and materials is endlessly fascinating. The inventors and manufacturers continue introducing products to make everything easier for people like you and me. They really want us to "do-it-ourselves."

Following is an introduction to tools and materials that will serve as a guide into this sometimes confusing world.

WHAT WOOD YOU LIKE TO KNOW?—
SOME 2 X 4 FACTS Wood that sits on the racks at the lumber yard waiting for you to buy it has two basic classifications, HARD and SOFT, depending on the type of tree it comes from. Softwoods come from trees that have cones—fir and pine. Hardwoods come from

trees that have leaves—oak, cherry, ash, etc.

I like to say that softwoods are easier to work with because they're soft and hardwoods are harder to work with because they're hard—hard to cut, hard to handle and hard to get. Unless you become a furniture or cabinet maker, most the projects you tackle will use softwoods.

Straight From The Sawmill Lumber, as it comes from the mill, is measured by its thickness and its width. The first dimension is always its thickness and the second, its width. So a 2 x 4 would seem to be two inches thick by four inches wide. But, like everything else in life, that isn't the whole story. 2 x 4 (or 1 x 3, 1 x 6, whatever) is what is called a *nominal* dimension and is really the size of the board before it's milled and finished. So children, a board that is called a 2 x 4 is actually 1' 1/2" x 3' 1/2". Go figure.

Obviously, this is pretty important stuff to know when you're building something and the measurements have to be exact. Just remember that what it's called isn't what it is.

HOLDING IT ALL TOGETHER: THE WONDERFUL WORLD OF FASTENERS

NAILS started to appear as soon as people learned to forge metals and there are a mind boggling number of varieties available. There still aren't many better ways to join things together as quickly and inexpensively. Here are the basics.

Common nails have heads and range from 1 to 6 inches in length. For some reason they are designated

SUSIE'S HELPFUL HINTS

Spend some time in the yard

Develop a relationship with a lumberyard that will allow you to choose the boards yourself. Look at each piece of lumber carefully. Be picky and don't settle for stuff you can't use. Careful selection will often allow you to step down a couple of grades and get lumber that will serve your project well.

in length by pennies—a three inch common for instance is called a 6 penny nail (6d). You can get a conversion chart at the hardware store until you get used to it. Used for rough carpentry.

Finishing nails have tiny heads and are used when a nail must be driven below the surface of the material with a "nail set" to hide it. They range from 1 to 4 inches in length.

Cut nails are made of steel and are flat instead of round. They are used to attach wood to masonry.

Cut flooring nails are flat as well and are used to attach floorboards to joists.

Fluted masonry nails have spirals running down the shaft. They attach wood to concrete blocks or brick walls.

Duplex nails have two heads and are used when something needs to be nailed securely but temporarily. They can be removed easily.

Brads are tiny nails with tiny heads for tiny jobs.

SCREWS Screws join materials with incredible strength. New technology and innovation in design have almost allowed the screw to replace the nail in many applications. They come in a wide range of shapes and sizes and have three basic head shapes: **Flat Head,** used when the screw must be flush to the surface; **Round Head,** used for materials that are too thin (less than 1/4 inch) to countersink (meaning to drive the screw below the surface of the material to hide it); **Oval Head,** a combination of flat and round head used when attaching metal to furniture. All these screws come in the traditional **slotted head** and **cross-slotted** or **"Phillips" head** design. Screwdrivers come with tips to fit the various heads, as do bits for drills.

The new kids on the block are **"Drywall"** screws. Originally designed for sheetrock and drywall, they are being used in many other applications. A cordless drill and a stash of drywall screws will solve a lot of home repair problems. A **Square Head** drywall screw in the shape of a finish nail is now available. It requires a special square head bit. The advantage is that you can drive the screw beneath the surface of the material.

WALL MOUNTINGS AND ANCHORS Once I got over the initial panic and the depression that followed my new shelves almost falling on Cindy's baby, I started to take a really close look at the gadgets that hold things on walls. What I discovered was a whole world of fasteners that will help you attach almost anything to almost anything else—from solid brick to hollow walls. And, when you're done, you can sleep secure in the knowledge that what you put up will stay up.

The key is to know the application and use the right fastener. By now, you should have a relationship with someone at a hardware store that you can go to fully armed with the right questions and come away with the right stuff.

Wall Plugs come in many shapes and sizes and are used in solid walls, although some will work well in sheetrock. The most common are **Molded Plastic, Extruded Plastic, Fiber, Extruded Aluminum,** and **Threaded Metal Plugs** made of aluminum. To use them, drill a hole with the proper bit into the surface, tap the plug into place, insert a screw and drive it home. They all work on the same principle, which is that they expand as the screw is sunk insuring a tight, secure fit.

Expansion Bolts are sometimes referred to as "thunderbolts" by carpenters because they are so strong. Basically they consist of a bolt in a threaded expander. You drill the hole, insert the expansion bolt and tap it home. Then you tighten the bolt to expand the casing. Once it's tight you can remove the bolt, hang whatever you're hanging and re-tighten it. They also come with hooks and eyes.

Hollow Wall Mountings including the famous **Molly bolt** are crafty little devices for hanging things on hollow walls. There are a zillion different kinds but they all operate on the same principle, which is that when inserted into the hole, the mechanism comes out the

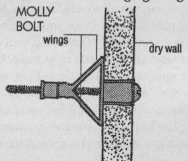

other side and expands against the back surface as the screw is tightened. The trick is to know the thickness of the wall so that the fastener you choose will go all the way through. If it doesn't, you can find yourself in the unpleasant position of having it stuck half way in and half way out.

Special Wall Plugs, Plastic Toggles, and **Collapsible Anchors** all open behind the wall when the screw or bolt is turned. **Gravity Toggles** and **Spring Toggles** both have arms or wings that catch against the interior wall. The weight of the wing on the gravity toggle causes it to fall after it's inserted. Spring toggles have spring-driven wings that pop open once they clear the hole on the other side.

Nylon Strap Toggles are relative newcomers in the hollow wall arena and I find them very easy to use. They come in different sizes and lengths.

> **IMPORTANT** You need to know the load you intend to place on anything you hang on a wall and choose the mounting device that is rated for the job. Check with your hardware person and read the manufacturer's instructions carefully. An ounce of prevention is worth a pound of cure.

PUTTING IT ALL TOGETHER: THE WONDERFUL WORLD OF TOOLS

If you go into the workshops of a dozen carpenters you'll see a dozen different ideas about what's necessary to get the job done. Over the years I've collected a set of tools that fits my needs to a tee. Of course, because I'm now a certified tool junkie, I'm adding to my stash all the time. If you purchase new tools on an as needed basis you'll be surprised at how quickly you'll fill up all of what you thought was that extra space in the corner of the basement.

The following wish list would provide you with the capability to do almost anything you choose.

POWER AND ELECTRIC TOOLS

IMPORTANT Power tools come with detailed instructions on how to use them and how to use them safely. Spend some time getting familiar with a new tool and practice with it before you jump into a task. The thing that initially most frightened me about them was the horrible noise they make. It takes some getting used to and a lot of carpenters wear special earplugs which block out the most irritating frequencies.

Belt Sanders make fast work of smoothing and finishing surfaces. Make sure it's easy to change the belts and the controls are accessible.

Circular Saws make cutting lumber and plywood a snap. With the right blades they can even cut metal. Using circular saws safely and efficiently requires practice. They are great, but require respect. Use a combination blade (one that cuts efficiently with or against the grain for most applications.)

Drills come in an astonishing variety of shapes and

SUSIE'S HELPFUL HINTS

When in doubt—rent

The tool rental business is booming. For relatively modest prices you can take home anything from a handsaw to a bulldozer. If you're approaching a project but don't feel like laying out the cash for a specialty item, or aren't sure if it's the tool for you, try it out as a rental and make the decision another time.

---

sizes. Choose one that is powerful but easy to handle. In my opinion one of your first purchases should be a quality cordless drill. It will become one of the most used tools in your workshop.

Glue guns heat several different kinds stick adhesives and feed them through a nozzle directly onto the work. They're great but can get messy.

Jigsaws are essential for fancy cutting and production work as well. With a simple change of blade they cut wood, metal, and plastic. They are easy to handle and if you purchase one with a variable speed motor, you have a very versatile addition to your kit.

Orbital sanders are designed for real finish work because the sandpaper moves in a circular motion and therefore won't scratch or gouge the surface of the work.

Staple guns, especially the electric or battery-operated kind, make working with fabric or screening a breeze. But a good hand-operated model will also do just fine.

Extension cords must be of good quality and rated at enough amperage to carry the load the power tools place on them. Brightly colored ones are best because they're easy to keep track of.

HAND TOOLS

Chisels require practice to use properly but they are an essential addition to the toolbox. They are necessary for mounting hinges and setting locks in doors as well as cleaning and shaping wood. They need to be kept sharp and clean. Carpenters judge their peers by the quality and the condition of their chisels. A good set of wooden-handled chisels makes a wonderful gift.

Files are great for getting into tight areas in woodworking as well as taking the rough edges off metal pipes. They also can be used to straighten the threads on a stripped bolt enough to allow you to remove a frozen nut. You should have a full, round, half round, and flat. A wooden handle with a metal insert completes the set.

Hammers come in lots of styles and weights. See what works for you. A sixteen-ounce claw hammer and a five ounce finish model for light work are enough to deal with most jobs.

Handsaws are a must just because you can't use a power saw for every job. Also, there is no better way to learn the basics of carpentry than by learning to use a handsaw. Ripsaws cut with the grain of the wood while the teeth of crosscut saws are designed to cut against the grain without leaving splinters or tearing the wood. Panel or dovetail saws have very fine teeth and although they cut slowly, they are very accurate and do the least damage to the wood. I recommend a combination handsaw. It will do a decent job of cutting with and against the grain.

Mallets are large-faced hammers with "soft" surfaces like cowhide, rubber or plastic. They are used with chisels so as not to damage the handle and also to nudge things into place that could be damaged with a steel hammer.

Mat knives are great multi-purpose cutting tools because the razor-style blades are very sharp and the models with retractable blades are safer to use than a regular razor knife.

Nail sets come in different sizes to fit the heads of different-sized finish nails. They are used to drive the head of the nail below the surface of the wood without damaging it. They are also called punches.

Planes are wood smoothing and shaping tools consisting of a sharp blade set in a "block" of metal or wood.

Pliers. There are a million different kinds and, in my opinion, you can't have enough—they do so many different things.

Putty knives come in a wide variety of shapes and sizes, they're great for filling holes and even scraping paint.

Screwdrivers. A complete kit should include a variety of sizes and lengths. Make sure you have slotted, Phillips and if you really want to be serious, hex and square heads. It's a good idea to have a slot-head screwdriver with a square shaft. If you're trying to remove or tighten a tough screw you can fix a crescent wrench on the shaft to add a little leverage. A battery-operated power model is very handy.

Snips are basically beefed up scissors. They have a spring in the handle and strong blades that allow you to cut things like sheet metal.

Wrenches come in all different shapes and sizes. Adjustable and slip-jaw styles serve a wide variety of basic needs. You will eventually want a small socket set and might even consider a power ratchet.

MEASURING AND LAYOUT TOOLS

Bevel gauges have an adjustable blade that allows you to mark or copy any angle.

Chalk lines are used to extend straight lines over long distances. String coated with chalk, usually blue, red or yellow, rolls out of a metal container. When the line is held taught and snapped, it leaves a marking line. Very useful for making cut marks on plywood. It also doubles as a plumb bob.

Clamps come in all shapes and sizes and they're the carpenter's third hand. "C" clamps do many different jobs, although you'll eventually need a set of pipe and T-Bar styles for holding large pieces.

Combination square One of the most useful tools in the box, this nifty item with its adjustable handle is a measuring, squaring, and leveling device. No shop should be without one.

Compasses are used for transferring very accurate measurements from one surface to another. Also, of course, to draw circles.

Framing squares make sure everything's in 90° alignment.

Lead pencils There are special carpenter's pencils that have wide flat leads which are good for marking and the pencil itself is flat so it won't roll off the table.

Levels are essentially straight boards with inset glass vials. The vials contain a bubble and are marked with two black lines in the center. When the bubble falls between the two lines whatever you're leveling is level. You'll want a small model called a torpedo and one at least two feet long, preferably longer for bigger jobs. Get models that have replaceable vials.

Miter boxes are used with fine tooth panel saws. A miter box guides the saw blade to help you cut angles accurately. They're essential if you're cutting molding or building picture frames.

Tape measures I like to have a couple of different sizes—a six-footer that I can carry to the store in my purse and a 25-footer with a 3/4 inch blade that I use for jobs around the house.

SPECIALITY ITEMS

Nail aprons hold pencils and nails but they also serve a safety function. They keep loose clothing from dangling over your work.

Dust masks and respirators We now know that some paints and adhesives are not meant to be inhaled on a regular basis and we must use masks and respirator as designated by the manufacturer.

Safety goggles are important because your eyes are important.

Tool belts are a third hand and a very convenient way to carry items you're using over and over again.

Work gloves are essential when handling rough lumber or pipe.

SUSIE'S HELPFUL HINTS

You've always got a tape measure

You just didn't know it. The good old American dollar may be shrinking with inflation but it still measures about six inches in length. In a pinch it'll give you a good guesstimate.

Workmates are a great invention—a truly portable workbench. They can be folded up and hung on the wall. The top is two thick pieces of plywood that become a vise by turning the handles at the base. Once you use one you'll wonder how you got along without it and it will serve you well until you're ready to build a workbench. They're sold everywhere.

PART TWO

COUNTING YOUR FINGERS:

THE OLDEST SAW IN CARPENTRY IS "SAFETY FIRST"

The resident woodworker in our community, Harvey, by name, was a wonderful gentle old man who seemed to really enjoy his work. He carried his tools in a beautiful wooden case that he had made to fit his needs and everything was in its proper place. There was always a smile on his face and he radiated such a sense of peace that when he was around even the kids were quiet. One day Timmy and I were watching him hang a new front door on our house. I told him how lucky we were to have him and asked how you could tell if someone was a good carpenter before you saw their work.

He put down his chisel and laughed. "One way I know for sure, Mrs. Tompkins, is if you're my age and you can count to ten on your fingers without using any of 'em twice, you're a good carpenter." It took me a second to realize what he meant and then it hit home. Harvey was saying that knowing the right and safe way to do things was as important as the finished product because it didn't matter that the door was a work of art if he hurt himself in the process of putting it up.

I offered him a cup of coffee and we talked. While I always had a secret interest in woodworking and carpentry, the power tools scared me to death and I was smart enough to know that you shouldn't use something you're afraid of. "Listen, Mrs. Tompkins," said Harvey, "there's two kinds of fear, the bad kind that freezes you up and gets you hurt and then there's the good kind, the kind that makes you pay attention. Me, I'm afraid in the good way every time I pick up a power saw. I use it because it makes for a better job. At the same time, I got a healthy respect for the fact that if I'm stupid with it, the darn thing'll put me out of work. Ain't a tool made that you can't learn to use, Mrs. Tompkins, if you learn to use it right and respect what it can do."

Later, he told me as he was packing up that if I really wanted to use woodworking tools, the first thing I should do was learn to cut a board with a handsaw and how to hammer a nail in straight. "It's just like with your boy here, Mrs. Tompkins. You've got to learn to crawl before you learn to walk."

I took his advice and, of course, he was right. I started out with a handsaw and today I'm skilled with all kinds of power tools. But every time I pick one up, I remember what he told me about respect and the "good kind of fear."

SOME SAFETY TIPS FROM THE PROS The more accomplished and confident you become, the more careful and aware you have to be. Why? The better you get, the less you feel you have to follow the rules. Overconfidence and carelessness often walk hand in hand. Follow these simple rules and you'll not only get the job done faster, you'll enjoy the finished product in one piece.

- Always unplug a power tool before changing the blade or making adjustments of any kind.
- Keep your work area clean and sawdust free. Sweep and clear scraps and debris off the floor frequently so there's nothing to stumble over while you're in the middle of a delicate operation.
- Make sure the circuits carry enough amps to handle the load your power tools put on the electrical system. And make sure the extension cord you're using is heavy duty as well. Don't run any power tool with household Zip cord.
- Learn to keep track of your extension cord while you're working so you don't accidentally cut it. The pros will often run it over their shoulder or hold it in their free hand so they know exactly where it is.
- Don't ever force a tool to do its work. If the blade jams or the drill freezes, shut it off and try again. Same goes with hand tools.
- Add a smoke detector to your work area.
- Keep a dry chemical fire extinguisher (2-A-ABC rating) handy. It will work on both combustible and electrical fires.
- Don't wear loose clothing or dangling jewelry. If

they get tangled in the tool you're in trouble.

- Before you use a tool of any kind, especially if you haven't used it for a while, check it carefully to make sure it's in good condition—the blades are sharp and tight, the cord is in good shape (no frays or cuts allowed) and the plug isn't broken or loose.

- The manufacturer put those pesky safety mechanisms there for a reason. Get used to it and learn to use them. Don't tamper with them or take them off.

- Wear safety goggles and masks when necessary. They take some getting used to but their value far outweighs the initial discomfort.

- Keep the kids well out of the way when you're using tools. Make it a rule and consider locking switches to keep the outlets around the workshop dead when you're not using them.

- If possible keep power tools locked away and hide the key.

- Make sure you have adequate light for the job. Arrange the work so no shadows are cast where you're cutting. Use clip-on lamps if necessary. SEEING IS SAFETY.

- If a tool breaks or a cord goes bad, mark it with tape so you'll remember to repair it.

- Use the right tool for the right job and study the manual that comes with it so you fully understand its capabilities and its limitations.
  Practice with new equipment on scrap lumber. Start with simple operations until you become comfortable.

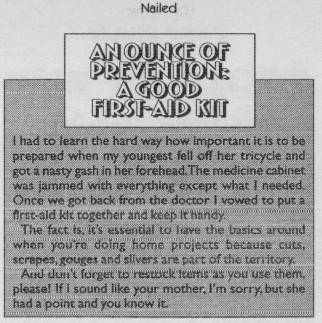

AN OUNCE OF PREVENTION: A GOOD FIRST-AID KIT

I had to learn the hard way how important it is to be prepared when my youngest fell off her tricycle and got a nasty gash in her forehead. The medicine cabinet was jammed with everything except what I needed. Once we got back from the doctor I vowed to put a first-aid kit together and keep it handy.

The fact is, it's essential to have the basics around when you're doing home projects because cuts, scrapes, gouges and slivers are part of the territory.

And don't forget to restock items as you use them, please! If I sound like your mother, I'm sorry, but she had a point and you know it.

PART THREE

TOOLS OF THE TRADE:

PACKING A POWER KIT THAT WORKS AS HARD AS YOU DO

When you really get into carpentry and home repair as I have, you'll begin to build a collection of tools that are going to need their own separate part of the house. Whether it's in the basement or the garage, you're going to need a work area for putting things together and storage of materials and power tools—that's right, your own workshop. You're also going to need a tool kit that holds the basics to do jobs around the house but isn't so heavy you need an assistant to drag it along.

Harvey's toolbox was simplicity itself. He didn't carry anything he wasn't going to use and, if he needed something special, he packed it for the job and put it back on the bench where it belonged when he was done. Toolboxes are like closets: they tend to collect odds and ends and fill up until you can't find anything you're looking for. It's frustrating and doesn't put you in a positive frame of mind for doing the job at hand.

There's a huge selection of toolboxes on the market with all kinds of drawers, compartments and lift-out trays. Some are gigantic and complex, others are so small they're more appropriate for the kids' lunch boxes than for holding tools. Professionals have tended to use metal boxes because of the constant beating they take on the job, but tougher plastic styles are on the market that do the job just as well and weigh a whole lot less. Make sure it's well constructed and has a large, sturdy handle. One of the things that makes a box hard to carry is a handle so thin it hurts your hand when you're hauling it around.

Here's what I carry in mine as a general rule:

(See: **Glossary** for definitions.)

I'm sure you've noticed that we've seen a lot of these tools before. If you pack your box with most or all of the above plus a couple of additions, you'll be prepared to tackle a minor plumbing or electrical job as well as a carpentry project. "Cross-over" and "Double-duty" are the watch words of the 90s— you're not only trendy but prepared as well.

HERE'S WHAT I CARRY IN MINE

- ☐ assortment of nuts, bolts, screws, nails, staples and washers
- ☐ blade screwdriver
- ☐ claw hammer (16 ounce)
- ☐ combination square
- ☐ crescent wrenches (two)
- ☐ electrician's tape
- ☐ flashlight
- ☐ florist's wire
- ☐ gents saw
- ☐ grounding adapter
- ☐ machinist's pliers
- ☐ masking tape
- ☐ mat knife and blades
- ☐ needle nose pliers
- ☐ pencils
- ☐ Phillips screwdriver
- ☐ slip-joint pliers
- ☐ socket set (small)
- ☐ tape measure
- ☐ torpedo level
- ☐ twine

PART FOUR

I CAN FIX THAT—

THE BASICS OF SIMPLE CARPENTRY AND REPAIRS

Here are some basics to help you get your feet wet and spread a little sawdust around the floor of your garage or basement.

CROSS-CUTTING YOUR FIRST BOARD WITH A HANDSAW Learning to use the handsaw will teach you a lot about wood and help you develop techniques and the confidence necessary when you move up to power tools.

The trick to cutting a piece of lumber is having a clearly marked cut line, knowing where the saw blade is and whether it cuts on the push or on the pull, using a firm, steady stroke and remembering to let the saw do the work. Sawing lumber is not an aerobic exercise.

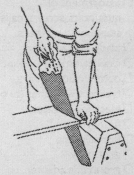

CROSS CUT
WITH HANDSAW

- Measure and mark the piece of lumber you
  want to cut and set it securely on a sawhorse
  or low bench.
- If you're right-handed, put your left knee up
  on the stock to hold it firmly in place and to
  get yourself out over the work for better
  leverage and balance.
- Hold the saw with your forefinger pointing
  toward the blade. This helps you keep the saw
  in line and will produce a straighter cut.
- Start the cut by drawing the saw back toward
  you several times, with light strokes to
  establish the "kerf" or cut.
- Continue cutting with slow, steady strokes,
  using the full length of the blade. When you
  are almost at the end, move your left hand
  over to hold the waste so that the last strokes
  won't break off the last layer of uncut wood.

HAMMERING A NAIL LIKE A PRO Tools were
developed to make things easier. One of the hardest
lessons to learn is to let the tool do the work. That's
why hammers come in different weights and sizes. If
you're using big nails it doesn't make sense to use a
tiny hammer. On the other hand a 20 ounce monster is
overkill when all you want to do is replace a small nail
(or brad) in the frame around Grandma's picture.

Pounding nails is an act of skill; it requires hand-eye
coordination, balance and rhythm. All you have to do
to master it is practice.

A nail will have a tendency to go into the wood in
the direction it's first set. So the first step is to set it cor-

HOW TO: KEEP A NAIL FROM SPLITTING THE WOOD

Nailing through thin lumber, especially near the edges, can cause the board to split and make you lose whatever hard work it's taken to get to that point. There are two solutions. First: pre-drill a hole of a smaller diameter than the nail and second: before you drive the nail into the board, blunt the pointed end with a few taps of your hammer.

rectly. If you want straight, set it straight. If it's going in at an angle, set it at the angle you want it to go.

The weight of the hammer's head is what drives the nail, not muscle power. I mean you have to hit it, but you don't have to beat it to within an inch of it's life to drive it home. The power and accuracy comes from your wrist.

Unless you're doing rough framing and it doesn't matter whether you damage the surface of the wood, you also have to know when to slow down and stop. If the surface shouldn't be marred, then stop before it's all the way home and finish the job with a nail set.

Short swings with a lot of wrist are the key. You have better control and far more accuracy. Also, keep your thumbs out of the way.

Nailed 99

DRILLING AND SCREWING When I was a child one of my uncles was a farmer, and one of his favorite possessions was his old model T Ford. Why? Because it was so simple to run and maintain and so versatile, that even when it stopped being a car it became the pump motor for his irrigation system. He loved it for the variety of tasks it would perform. I love drills for the same reason.

They do so much and they're so easy to use. I have a heavy duty 3/8" electric combination drill and a powerful cordless model with several attachments and I use them both constantly. In fact, adding a screwdriver bit to my cordless drill makes it such an effective tool that it's replaced my hammer in lots of joining applications.

The modern drill does more than just cut little holes. With the proper attachments it becomes: a screwdriver, a sander, polisher, circular saw, hedge trimmer, paint stirrer, jigsaw, sump pump, grinder and probably several more things I don't know about, but will buy as soon as I do.

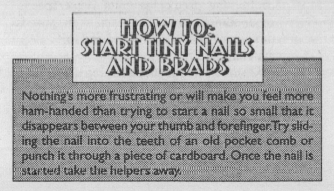

HOW TO: START TINY NAILS AND BRADS

Nothing's more frustrating or will make you feel more ham-handed than trying to start a nail so small that it disappears between your thumb and forefinger. Try sliding the nail into the teeth of an old pocket comb or punch it through a piece of cardboard. Once the nail is started take the helpers away.

SUSIE'S HELPFUL HINTS

New screws in old holes

If you find the need to put a new screw in an existing hole, use one that's longer and thicker so it will thread its way into fresh wood—just make sure the new one isn't too long for the material. Otherwise you'll find the point coming out the other side.

A second option is to drill out the hole to a larger size and tap in a piece of dowel that has been coated with carpenter's glue. You can also try filling the existing hole with wooden match sticks or toothpicks or stuff some steel wool into the opening.

CHOOSING THE DRILL THAT'S RIGHT FOR YOU

There are so many features available on modern electric and cordless drills that you would do well to shop around for features before you buy. Although most modern drills are cased in plastic anyway, you should make sure that the drills you choose have non-conducting plastic bodies.

- Variable speed is the only way to go, meaning that finger pressure on the trigger of the drill controls the speed of the motor. Slower speeds produce more turning force and higher speeds produce cleaner holes in wood and soft materials.
- Make sure the trigger has a locking device that will allow you to run the drill without having to press the trigger. This is valuable when you are using sanding or polishing attachments.
- The "chuck" size of the drill is the limitation on the shaft size of bits the drill will accept. For most home applications a 3/8" chuck is more

than adequate. Some chucks are self-
tightening, meaning they don't need a
chuck key to tighten the bit into the chuck.

WHAT TO DO WHEN THEY WON'T UNSCREW

Eventually you're going to face one of the fixer-upper's
biggest headaches—a screw that needs to come out but
won't. One of the unwritten rules of home repair is that
the screw that's stuck or frozen is the last one left.
Fortunately, there are some tricks of the trade and hope-
fully one of them will work. Patience is the key here. Work
slowly and notice what's happening. Don't force it,
because if you damage the slot you'll have to drill the
screw out with a bigger bit. It's a pain in the neck.

If the slot of the screw is filled with paint or plaster, use
the edge of your screwdriver to chip it out and tap the
head gently to loosen the paint around the edges. If it's a
Phillips type use an ice pick or a finish nail to dig out the
paint.

Sometimes the slot of the screw is too narrow for the
blade of your screwdriver. If that's the case use your hacksaw and try to widen and deepen it.

If you can move the screw but it stops after less than a
full turn, try working it back and forth in tiny turns until
the screw frees itself.

Set the screwdriver in the slot and tap it gently with
your hammer. The shock may loosen it up enough to get
it out.

If the screw comes out part way but gets stuck, take your
lock-joint pliers and clamp them firmly on the screw head.
It should give you the leverage you need to finish the job.

- When you're drilling into dense materials like brick or masonry, having a combination drill with a hammer function like I do is a real work saver. While the bit turns it also goes back and forth, pounding away at the material as it cuts the hole.

- There is absolutely no reason to buy a drill that isn't reversible, meaning that the motor turns the chuck in either direction. This is invaluable because with the addition of a screwdriver bit, your drill will set and remove screws.

- Before you buy a drill, hold it in your hand to make sure it fits and feels properly balanced. Also, the drill of your dreams should have the ability to add an extra handle on the side. This will allow for more sure gripping and leverage if you're pushing into something hard.

- Invest in a carrying case for your drill. It'll hold attachments and help keep track of bits.

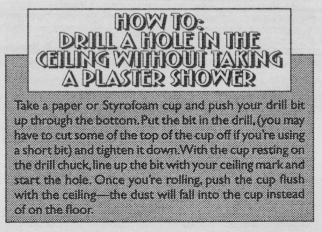

HOW TO:
DRILL A HOLE IN THE CEILING WITHOUT TAKING A PLASTER SHOWER

Take a paper or Styrofoam cup and push your drill bit up through the bottom. Put the bit in the drill, (you may have to cut some of the top of the cup off if you're using a short bit) and tighten it down. With the cup resting on the drill chuck, line up the bit with your ceiling mark and start the hole. Once you're rolling, push the cup flush with the ceiling—the dust will fall into the cup instead of on the floor.

USING POWER SAWS WITH CONFIDENCE

Control is the issue when learning to use power saws. That means you're familiar with the tool, not only in terms of how it operates and what its safety features are, but also that you have set up your work space so that you are in total command and there won't be any surprises when the motor's roaring and the sawdust's flying.

Read the manuals thoroughly and practice the cutting and safety tips they give you before you tackle projects. The manual will also tell you how to maintain the tool and how to spot things that need repair or adjustment.

> **IMPORTANT** Never set a power saw down until the blade's stopped turning.

Circular saws are heavy and may feel awkward until you get used to them. Jigsaws are much lighter and easier to control so I recommend gaining skill and confidence with a jigsaw before trying a circular saw.

> **IMPORTANT** Always make sure the tool is in good working order and that the blade is sharp.

Jigsaws do many cutting operations because you can fit them with a wide variety of blades. They are as at home with metal and pipe as they are with wood. Wide blades insure straighter cuts, narrow blades will cut tight curves. Choose the right blade for the job. The key with any power saw is to let it do the work.

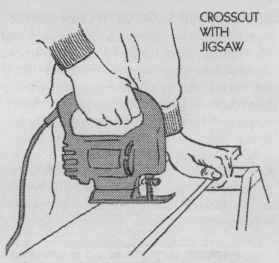

CROSSCUT
WITH
JIGSAW

Don't push the tool and you'll be pleased with the results.

Circular saws also come with a wide variety of cutting blades. The standard for most operations in wood is a combination blade since it will allow you to cut along and against the grain with a minimum of splinters. Eventually, you'll find yourself changing blades to suit the job, but in the beginning keep it simple. Carpenters usually use circular saws with blades in the 6 to 7 1/4 inch range. They are powerful and accurate. I think, for most of the work you'll be doing, a saw with a 4 1/2 inch blade is the answer. They are smaller, lighter and, although not as powerful, will handle wood up to the 2 inch range with ease.

Circular saws cut upwards, meaning the blade is cutting from the bottom of the wood to the top. The reason you need to know this is that the cleanest or "finish" cut will be on the bottom of the material. You need to decide which side of the work is going to be the top and measure and mark cut lines accordingly.

Learning to use power saws is essential if you intend to attempt bigger and bigger projects. If you respect them and learn to use them nothing is out of your reach.

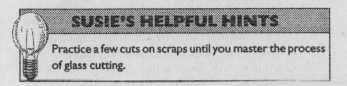

SUSIE'S HELPFUL HINTS

Practice a few cuts on scraps until you master the process of glass cutting.

A NEW WINDOW DOESN'T HAVE TO BE A PANE

If you've got kids, eventually you're also going to have to deal with broken glass. But there's nothing easier than replacing a window panel, or a glass panel in a cabinet door. The tools you'll need are a glass cutter, a board to use as a straight edge, a framing square, tape measure, light machine oil, a pair of pliers, a putty knife, glazing compound, glazier's points and a brush to sweep away little chips of glass.

Preparing The Opening

- Put on a pair of gloves, grab the pliers and clean the remaining shards out of the opening.
- Take a putty knife and chip all the glazing compound from the frame and clean the opening. If your window has a rubber gasket, remove it to reuse later.
- Measure the opening to get cutting measurements. When you measure the

glass for cutting, the dimensions will be 1/8th of an inch smaller than the opening so the pane will fit easily into it.

Cutting The Glass

- Lay the glass on a padded surface and butt the straight edge up to its base.
- Lay the framing square on the glass where you want the first cut to be and butt it up to the straight edge as well to hold it in place.
- Dip the glass cutter in the oil and score the glass by running the cutter along the edge of the framing square using light pressure and a fluid movement. All you want to do is "score" or mark the break line on the surface of the glass. Only one pass per cut please.
- Turn the pane over and tap the cut line with the end of the glass cutter. Leave the score mark side underneath.
- Wearing your gloves, snap the glass along the cut line. Always press down. Sometimes it helps to place the glass on your straight edge board, lining the edge up to the score line.
- Use the breaker notches on the glass cutters or a pair of pliers to snap off any ragged edges.
- Cut the other dimension and you're ready to install.

Installing The New Window Pane

- Set the pane in the opening to make sure it fits.
- At this point, if your window uses a rubber gasket instead of glazing compound, replace

the gasket and you're finished. If not, proceed.

- Run a thin line of "bedding" putty around all four sides of the opening and press the pane into place.

REPLACING WINDOWS

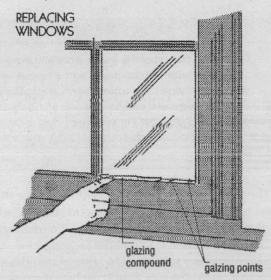

glazing compound

galzing points

- Set glazing points every 4 to 6 inches to hold the window in place. Use a putty knife to press them in about half way and tap gently with a hammer to drive them home.
- Roll the glazing compound into a rope about 3/8th of an inch in diameter and run it around the window. Press it down and then run a putty knife or glazier's knife to form a triangular bead. Clean up the excess and allow it to dry for a week before painting.

THE CASE FOR BOOK SHELVES As I discovered
early on, putting up a set of shelves is a great way to
learn several basic skills. Shelves involve a little sawing, a little drilling, a little leveling and a lot of
thought.

SUSIE'S HELPFUL HINTS

Go to your local sporting goods store and buy a clear
plastic box with compartments and a hinged lid that
snaps securely shut. The trout fishermen who use them
think they were designed to hold flies and weights and
arcane things like that, but I'm convinced they were really
made for keeping loose hardware organized in your traveling
tool kit.

There are several issues to deal with. First, the shelves
have to stay up. Second, they have to be installed correctly and have to be level and square. Third, they have
to hold the intended load without sagging.

Sagging occurs when the shelving material is asked
to span a greater unsupported distance than its thickness will allow. The rule of thumb is that a 1 inch shelf
needs supports every three feet in order to remain
straight and that the supports, even on a short shelf
should be inset from the ends at least 6 to 8 inches to
balance the load.

In order for the shelves to be installed correctly you
need to know the surface you're mounting them on.
As we know, brick, solid walls, and hollow walls all
have different fastening requirements.

In our example, we're going to mount four 1 x 8 x 35

inch shelves using one of the most common shelving systems—"standard and bracket" onto a 5/8" inch sheet rock wall.

Standard and bracket systems consist of standards which are slotted metal channels of varying lengths and shelf brackets with hooks that lock into the slots. The slots are spaced up and down the length of the standard to make the shelving fully adjustable. The standards have mounting holes drilled every 12 inches to mount them on the wall.

The Materials List

1—1 x 8 x 12 feet long, clear pine lumber
2—metal standards 48" long
8—8" shelf brackets
8—2" plastic anchors with 2" inch screws

The Tool List

Drill with masonry bit
Two foot level
Hammer
Pencil
Nail set
Tape measure
Crosscut hand saw (or circular, or jigsaw)
Combination square
Screwdriver

THE PROJECT

Cut the shelves from the 1 x 8 x 12 board.

Set up your sawing area so you have room to work. Take the combination square and check the end of the board to be sure it's square. If it isn't your first cut will be to square it up.

From the square end measure 35 inches and draw a cut line. Cut the first shelf, remember to hold the work as you come to the finish of the cut so it won't break off. Continue measuring and cutting until you have four shelves.

At this point you can take the time to sand the edges and ends of the shelves to clean them up and remove rough edges and splinters. If they're going to be painted or stained, this is the time to do it.

Mount The Standards Once you've decided where the shelves are going to go and how high you want the tallest shelf, you're ready to mount the first standard.

Place the standard against the wall so that the highest point is at least 6 inches above the last shelf. Holding the standard against the wall, take the nail set and push it through one of the mounting holes near the center of the standard—it doesn't matter which one—and put enough pressure on it to make a mark on the wall. Set the standard aside and punch the mark just a little deeper so you've got a guide for the drill bit.

Using the masonry bit (you've already made sure it's the right size for the screws) drill the first hole. If you have a variable speed drill, start at a lower speed to make sure you won't stray from the mark (carpenters say the drill is "walking" when this happens) and go for it.

Tap the plastic anchor gently into the hole. Get the standard, a screwdriver and screw.

Insert the screw into the same hole you used to mark the wall, set the screw into the anchor and gently screw it in until the standard is against the wall but still loose enough to move.

Take your level and hold it against the standard, moving the standard until the little bubble shows that the standard is perfectly level, and mark the remaining holes.

Swing The Standard Swing the standard aside so you can get to the marks. Now drill and fit the remaining anchors. Swing the standard back into place and screw it in.

Now you need to measure for the second standard. If our shelves are 35" long and we need them to overhang at least 6" on each side we subtract 12 from 35 and discover that the second standard has to be approximately 23 inches from the one we've already mounted. Measure over and make a mark.

What now you ask? Well, a few installations down the line you probably can do the next step by yourself, but for now get one of the kids or even George to help out.

Pick a place on the standard you've mounted on the wall and hook in a bracket. Place the loose bracket next to it, line it up, count the slots and hook a bracket in the same place on the loose one.

Move the loose standard over to the 23" mark and have your worthy assistant grab a shelf. While you hold the bracket in place have your assistant set the shelf on the brackets and then place the level on the shelf. Adjust the shelf until it's level and mark the wall.

You're Almost Done Repeat the steps above to mount the second standard, space and mount the brackets (you may have to tap them gently with a hammer to seat them), set the shelves in place and you're done.

Your shelves should be sturdy, level and secure. Now you can stuff them with books.

Congratulations! You're on the way to becoming a true Fixer.

LEVELING
A SHELF

SECTION FOUR:

GETTING THE PICTURE

TAKE A LITTLE KNOWLEDGE, ADD A PHONE AND YOU CAN MAKE SIMPLE APPLIANCE AND ELECTRONIC REPAIRS THAT WILL SAVE TIME AND MONEY

We'd been at the school picnic for about ten minutes when my oldest son crept up behind me and caught me red-handed. I was bragging about the latest repair I had made on our basement refrigerator, once again saving us the cost of replacing it unnecessarily. Later, he and the rest of my family teased me about it, but underneath it all they were proud of me and my ability to keep appliances going around the house long after other families have given up and replaced them.

Actually, I don't consider it bragging, but a significant public service for my gender to pass on some vital information that every woman should know. Here's what happened. We keep a fairly ancient GE refrigerator in the basement that we use for the endless overflow from our kitchen refrigerator. Anyway, one day I noticed a loud clicking sound from the back of the freezer compartment. I called a repairman, who said the service call would be $60 plus any parts and the labor to install them. Reluctant to sink a $100 or more into an antique that I probably couldn't give away, I hung up.

Then I noticed in the Yellow Pages that GE had an 800 number. I called and got something called the answer line. After I fetched the model number of the refrigerator, I was connected to a very nice man who listened carefully as I described the problem and then told me it was probably the small fan that circulates cold air. He explained exactly how I could inspect the fan, which involved removing five screws.

Sure enough, the fan had a broken blade. I called back and ordered the part, which came to about $8. Two days later, the part arrived along with a four-page illustrated instruction book on how to take out the old fan and put the new one in. The whole process took me 20 minutes, for which I "earned" about $117.

Since that day, I've become a devotee of 800 numbers. Almost every appliance and electronic company has someone you can talk to. As often as not, I have a problem that I can't fix myself. But even in those cases, the customer service representative has given me some ideas about what the problem is and what the parts should cost. I sound like an expert when I call a repairman, and, if they know that I know, I'm a lot less likely to get hammered by the repair bill.

Appliances, both large and small, are the modern family's workhorses. But, unfortunately, we tend to take them for granted. Preventive maintenance and simple repairs can save you a lot of money and often eliminate the emergency shut downs that are so frustrating and time consuming—not to mention expensive.

PART ONE

AN ABUNDANCE OF REPAIR
AND MAINTENANCE
INFORMATION IS
AVAILABLE BY PHONE

Of all the marketing pitches to which we consumers are subjected, I think the most bizarre are appliance and electronic service contracts. Think about it: a salesman has no sooner finished spending an hour telling you what a technological wonder your new TV set is then he launches into an equally passionate argument that you should fork over another $125 to make sure someone will fix it when it breaks. I must admit that on rare occasions I've been talked into signing one of these documents, and as the time starts to run out, I find myself hoping that the thing will blow up so all my money won't go down the drain.

But, for a moment, let's put emotions aside and take a look at the facts. Does it pay to purchase a service contract? According to every study I've ever examined, the answer is a resounding NO! In fact, the appliance companies make a huge profit on them, which is why your salesman puts forth such an impassioned sales argument.

This pitch is made up of two basic points. First, if you have a problem you can call us and we'll come out right away. Second, repairs can be expensive, and with the service contract you don't pay a cent (they mean, an additional cent on top of the dollars you've already spent.)

AGA	800-633-2242
AMANA	800-843-0304
BRAUN INC.	800-272-8611
CALORIC	800-511-3195
DELONGHI AMERICA	800-322-3848
EUREKA	800-282-2686
FRIGIDARE	800-444-4944
GENERAL ELECTRIC	800-432-2737
GIBSON APPLIANCE	800-444-4944
GM SERVICE CENTER	800-654-5450
HALLOCK'S (MAYTAG)	800-462-9824
IN-SINK-ERATOR (EMERSON)	800-421-5111
JENN-AIR	800-346-8481
KELVINATOR	800-444-4944
KITCHENAID	800-442-1111
MAGIC CHEF	800-772-7021
MAGNAVOX	800-242-9225
PHILLIPS	800-242-9225
RCA	800-643-4474
ROPER	800-442-1111
SEARS ROEBUCK	800-248-0696
SYLVANIA	800-242-9225
TAPPAN	800-444-4944
TECHNICS	800-545-2672
WESTINGHOUSE	800-444-4944
WHIRLPOOL	800-442-1111

Argument one doesn't hold water in almost all areas of the country. My phone book has pages of appliance repair companies and regardless of what the salesman says, all companies will fix their own products, service contract or no service contract.

Argument two has some merit—so why don't you set up your own

BOOKLETS
IN A BOX

One afternoon I was chatting with a young lady, who
sold me a dehumidifier, about how hard it was to keep
track of all the receipts for all the household items we
owned. Just a couple weeks before, I'd torn the entire
house apart trying to find the receipt for an answering
machine I was sure was under warranty. Without the
receipt, I couldn't prove when I bought it. She suggested something so obvious that it verged on the bril-
liant—staple the sales receipt to the inside cover of the
instruction book and file it away. It struck me that her
solution killed two birds with one stone, not only could
I keep track of the receipts, but of the books as well.

I bought a file box and stored everything in alphabet-
ical order. Now when there's a problem either with a
repair or warranty issue or I know exactly where to
look for answers. It's saved me hours of frustration.

self-service contract? I use this formula: I always ask
the price of a service contract, then put one-third of it in
a special repair account. The special account hasn't
always covered all of my repair costs, but the more preventive maintenance I do (and the better I get at shopping for repair services), the larger my balance gets.

And 800 telephone calls are free. On the previous
page are some 800 numbers for major appliance mak-
ers to get you started. The instruction manuals and
product information that come with your appliance
will also have lots of access numbers and help-line
procedures. So does the phone book. Take advantage
of them.

TOOLS OF THE TRADE:

EVERYTHING YOU NEED FOR SIMPLE APPLIANCE AND ELECTRONIC REPAIRS

There's one way in which maintaining electronic equipment is exactly like raising kids—you've got to keep their heads clean. None of us would dream of sending our children to school or to bed with a milk mustache or chocolate streaks on the cheeks. Now, I've saved myself a lot of money and grief by keeping my electronic equipment clean, too.

I learned the secret when the most awful of awful tragedies struck my family—the Nintendo machine wouldn't work. Flip in a game, and all you saw was a black, flashing screen. The withdrawal tremors were so severe that after listening to the shrieking for twenty minutes, I grabbed the machine and dashed over to the place where my kids buy used video games. The nice young man behind the counter listened for a second, grabbed a little flat stick with a white pad on the end, put a few drops of fluid on the pad, then inserted the stick into the Nintendo. He rubbed for a couple minutes, and pulled out the stick.

The pad was black, and for a moment I felt as embarrassed as if he'd yelled, "Ring around the collar." Then he told me that dust gets into the machine even in the cleanest of houses (a category into which mine doesn't fit). For a few dollars, he sold me a cleaning kit that has kept the Nintendo (and Genesis and Super Nintendo) working perfectly.

I discovered that anything else that plays a tape has to be cleaned, too—the VCR, answering machine, tape player, car stereo, etc. In fact, I suspect I dumped a malfunctioning answering machine that probably only needed a good cleaning. Now I have a little store of kits and cleaning supplies for the various electronic items we keep around the house.

YOU'VE PROBABLY GOT A LOT OF WHAT YOU NEED

If you've been building a basic tool kit to deal with carpentry, plumbing and electrical projects around the house, you've got what you need to tackle simple appliance maintenance and repair. Electronic problems, on the other hand, can be more difficult—there aren't that many moving parts and the engineering of these systems is complex. Beyond the obvious problems with cords and external damage, most internal work, with the exception of cleaning and general maintenance, is best left to the pros.

PART THREE

I CAN FIX THAT—

APPLYING YOURSELF TO APPLIANCES

I live in the New England countryside and that means lots of trees, so it's not uncommon for us to lose power during a storm. Although I realize this is a price we have to pay for watching deer graze in the front yard, it's inconvenient and annoying. Last Christmas, I also learned it can be expensive.

I was in the kitchen preparing Christmas Eve dinner for my family and a gaggle of relatives when the house went dark. The timing couldn't have been worse, but we eventually carted everything to my mother-in-law's house. The problem was that, as usual, I couldn't remember exactly what appliances I had on when the power went off. That means being awakened by bright lights and a blasting stereo when the power comes back on at 3:00 a.m. But this time, the power came back on with a surge that blew out some very expensive part of our 25″ color television set.

I was cursing my memory when my friendly repairman introduced me to surge suppressors. These devices are long metal boxes with a row of out-

lets for plugging in electronic equipment and appliances. Not only do they eliminate the need for a nest
of extension cords, but they also stop power surges
before they can damage your equipment.

To my dismay, I learned I could have enough
surge suppressors to equip our entire neighborhood
for what my TV repair cost. That's the preventive
part of Preventive Maintenance. But I learned my
lesson and so should you.

There are a lot of simple repairs and maintenance
projects that you can tackle right now and the more
you do the more complex the tasks you can undertake.

ELIMINATING PRESSING PROBLEMS
WITH YOUR IRON
Your electric iron takes a lot of lit-
tle electrons dancing through the circuit to make it
work and, therefore, puts heavy demands on your system. Usually, the manufacturer does not recommend
using an extension cord and I don't either. Set up near
enough to an outlet to do the job without needing one.
But no matter what you do, eventually something will
go wrong. The iron won't get hot, or it'll heat so slowly you could finish the crossword before you can finish
a blouse. Maybe it gets hot but no steam pours out of
the little holes. Whatever it is, you've got a problem
and, before you rush down to the mall, it's worth looking into as a potential in-home repair.

The rules and logic that apply to tracking a problem in one kind of hand-held small appliance are
pretty much the same as for larger ones. Start by eliminating the obvious and work toward the obscure.

First, check the circuits to make sure you aren't

SUSIE'S HELPFUL HINTS

Clogged steam vents

If the steam vents are clogged, clean them with a piece of wire or a paper clip. Fill the iron with a mixture of half white vinegar and half water and set it on a rack over your broiler pan. Turn it on and let it steam until all the solution is gone, then run the iron at high temperature for 30 minutes to an hour.

To clean the bottom plate, use dishwashing detergent and a little baking soda. If the plate is metal and develops scratches that catch on clothing, try rubbing it gently with very fine steel wool. (DON'T TRY THIS ON A NON-STICK SURFACE.)

If you live in an area with very hard water consider using distilled water for steam ironing.

overloading. If overloading isn't the problem, then you've got a fault in the iron itself or a bad power cord.

When you use an iron you put a lot of stress on the cord and you should inspect it frequently for frays and cracks. A damaged cord will not allow the iron to heat fully or can make it heat slowly. The cord is often the culprit.

If you're like me, no matter how many times you remind yourself that it's bad to unplug something by yanking the cord out of the wall, sometimes it happens and after a while the plug and its connection will be damaged.

Replacing one appliance's power cord is pretty much like replacing another. Sometimes it's really easy; for instance—when the cord has a male on one end and a female on the other and there's an outlet in the appliance for it to plug into. But a lot of appli-

IRON

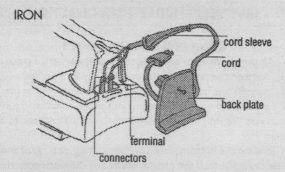

cord sleeve
cord
back plate
terminal
connectors

ances are designed with the connection inside. Your trusty manual will contain a diagram that shows how the cord is connected and where.

Remove the cord from the appliance and use your continuity tester to check that there aren't any broken wires in the cord itself. Snap the alligator clip onto one of the prongs of the plug and touch the probe to the other. If the light comes on there's a short. If the light doesn't come on it's time to check the cable. Clip onto one of the wires and touch the probe to one of the prongs, then the other. The light should come on when you're touching the prong that's connected to the wire you're clipped to. Test the other prong and other wire. No light means a break in the cable. Get an exact replacement, hook it up and get back to ironing.

If the cord is working properly, however, the problem is in the appliance. While you can inspect it for obvious damage and faults, the best thing to do is take it to the repair shop.

DON'T GIVE YOUR FRIDGE THE COLD SHOULDER

One of the biggest money savers in the Fix-It arena is preventive maintenance—you know, eliminating huge dollar repairs by taking care of little things before they get out of hand. I'm going to keep saying this until you listen or go mad. Since I started taking care of things around the house I've come to realize that since we've invested so much hard-earned money in our major and minor appliances it's foolish not to keep them in top shape.

We really have to remember that things were never intended to last forever and no matter how bulky and solid a refrigerator or freezer may seem, it's like everything else—occasionally it needs a little love, affection, and personal attention.

Here are some tips for making sure the milk stays cold, but remember to unplug the beast before you work on it.

At least once, but preferably, twice a year clean the condenser coils. They're located either underneath, in which case you can pull off the bottom grill and get to them, or behind. If they're behind, you'll have to pull the monster away from the wall. If you're lucky it's on wheels. In either case, use the crevice tool on your vacuum cleaner to suck out the dust and any thing else that may have found it's way back there—in my house that's usually loose change and expired grocery

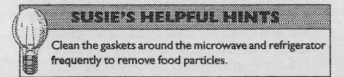

SUSIE'S HELPFUL HINTS

Clean the gaskets around the microwave and refrigerator frequently to remove food particles.

SUSIE'S HELPFUL HINTS

A noisy refrigerator is really irritating. Sometimes the problem is that the unit isn't level. Make the adjustments and you've got a good chance of a little quiet on the home front.

coupons along with some hard candy and a couple of withered orange peels.

If you're the proud owner of a self-defrosting model you'll have to clean the drainage system. Assuming you can find your way around the food, you'll see that little plugs cover the drain holes which are found at the bottom of the freezer and refrigerator sections. Pull them out and if necessary, unclog them with a piece of wire stiff enough to do the job. Finish off by flushing the system with a turkey baster filled with warm water and dump the drain pan.

If you find water collecting under your refrigerator, it's possible that the drain pan needs replacing or that the drain hose, if you have one, leaks. Both items are easily replaced.

If the fridge is doing its job of keeping things cold and frozen, and if it doesn't need defrosting, check the following:

- that the temperature controls are set properly.
- that the condenser coils are clean and free of obstructions.
- that none of the seals leak. Air leaks in the rubber gaskets that are supposed to keep the door tightly shut and sealed will really affect the refrigerator's ability to keep things cold because they allow frost to build up in the freezer section and therefore

inhibit cooling.
- that the refrigerator is level from side to side and tilted slightly back so that the door will not only close by itself but stay shut.

SUSIE'S HELPFUL HINTS

Let glass shelves from your refrigerator warm up to room temperature before you wash them. They won't crack. For really hard to remove stains inside your microwave bring a cup of water to boiling inside and wipe the loosened crud away.

Leveling Most refrigerators have leveling screws or legs in the front. To set them properly, all you need is your two foot level and a block of wood that's thick enough to get the front of the unit off the ground while you set the feet.

Tilt it back and set the block so both feet are off the ground. Make sure the block's wedged in there securely so a large white object full of heavy food doesn't fall on your fingers.

Place the level on one side of the refrigerator and look at the bubble to see which way it is leaning. If you pull the top of the level away from the side, keeping the bottom touching you can get an idea of how far it's out of level.

SUSIE'S HELPFUL HINTS

No leaks please!

It's really important to check the bases of appliances that use water because, over time, leaks will cause the floor to rot, and that's a big and unnecessary repair bill.

Adjust the feet by screwing them up or down until the unit is level side to side. Usually the levelers will raise the unit when turned counterclockwise and lower it the other way.

Make sure the refrigerator tips slightly backwards; just enough so that gravity will help the door shut easily on its own. You can do this by raising **both** leveling feet proportionally to raise the front without affecting the level side to side.

Sagging Doors The bad news is that even on the sturdiest of models, after a few years the screws that hold the hinges in place will loosen and the doors will start to sag. The good news is that it's an easy fix. The top hinge is usually covered by a plastic cap, unless the kids have used it for a hockey puck. Pop it off and you'll see an adjustable hinge with two screws. (If your model has a top freezer compartment, you'll

LEVELING
REFRIGERATOR

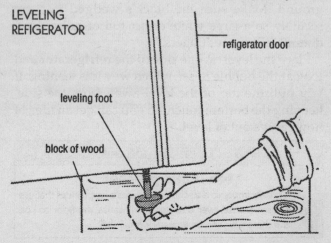

refigerator door

leveling foot

block of wood

have to remove the freezer door to work on the lower one. Think of this as a good excuse to defrost.) Loosen the screws so you can shift the door back into place and hold it while you tighten them back up. While you're at it, check the door gasket for cracks and gaps. Often a gasket will go bad because the door is out of line.

SUSIE'S HELPFUL HINTS

Keep the gaskets on the refrigerator and dishwasher doors flexible by rubbing them with a little mineral oil or Vaseline.

DON'T COME UNPLUGGED
WHEN THE DRYER DOESN'T DRY
One of the major causes of poor drying is lint, which, like the pesky commodity that it is, hides in several places. Most obvious, of course, is the lint filter, which should be cleaned after every use. But the stuff will also collect in the exhaust duct so it's a good idea to remove the duct once a year and shake it out. While you've got it off, take a coat hanger and clean the vent tube that connects you to the great outdoors and remove anything that's collected in the damper outside. Make sure that the vent hose doesn't have any low spots or sags that can trap lint and even water from condensation. When it comes time to replace the duct, you can buy flexible tubing that isn't pleated like an accordion and won't allow as much stuff to collect.

If you have a gas dryer, occasional maintenance will mean fewer visits from the serviceman. Check the pilot light frequently—sometimes it will go out. The service manual has good, clear instructions for how to relight it. Occasionally, you will want to unplug or switch off the power to the dryer and remove the front panel that covers the burner assembly so you can wipe it clean with a rag. Then vacuum the area with a crevice tool to remove debris.

Poor Heating When the dryer doesn't seem to be heating, there's a good chance that the air/gas mixture is out of adjustment. Look at the flame with the dryer running. If it's yellow and roars like a wounded lion, you've got a problem that should be placed in the hands of a competent repairman.

MAKING YOUR DISHWASHER HAPPY Did you know that you use less water to run a dishwasher than you do when the dishes are done by hand? George and the kids loved to hear that one. The truth is, dishwashers are a major convenience and, after years of resistance, I can't believe how I ever got along without one. However, they do require a little TLC to keep the silver gleaming and the spots off the glasses.

If you're getting a dishwasher installed for the first time, it's a good idea to run a snake through the drain line that you're hooking it into. A clogged drain will take care of sink water for some time without appearing blocked, but when you add the rush of water that

---

SUSIE'S HELPFUL HINTS

Don't use abrasive cleaners on the surfaces of appliance control panels. They will scratch the plastic. Warm soapy water is the best solution.

SUSIE'S HELPFUL HINTS

If your detergent is old and lumpy it may not be dissolving fully and won't have the clout to clean your dishes. I've found that dishwashing detergent has a very short shelf life and that it doesn't pay to keep it around it large quantities even if it seems cheaper at the time when you're comparing prices in the supermarket.

comes from an emptying dishwasher, there's a good chance the drain will overflow. The good news is, because of the high water pressure needed to run the cycle and the fact that the waste water ejected by a dishwasher is hot, a well snaked line will probably never clog again.

Remember that no matter how hot your water seems, it's not hot enough to sterilize dishes. The temperature necessary to sterilize things is 180° or more and that temperature is dangerous in a home where people are turning on the hot taps to take showers and wash hands. The proper range, as we know, is between 130° and 140°F. Don't be tempted to turn it up.

Some common problems:

The Dishwasher Doesn't Fill Simple things first, as usual. Make sure the water is turned on. If that isn't the problem, grab the manual and find the diagram of the dishwasher's insides. Find the location of the float and check to see if it's stuck. Lift it out and look for things that may have fallen into the opening.

Check the inlet screen valve and see if it's clogged.

SUSIE'S HELPFUL HINTS

Feeding the seals

Dishwashers keep a certain amount of water in the bottom to insure that the rubber O-rings and seals stay wet. If the water evaporates for any reason, the seals will dry out and the pump will freeze up or start to leak. If you're going to be away from the house for a period of time, pour a little mineral oil in the bottom of the dishwasher. The oil will float on top of the water and it won't evaporate.

The Dishwasher Doesn't Drain See if the drain filter is clogged. Also, look at the strainer, the pump, and the drain valve. Lastly, make sure the drain hose isn't looped or kinked.

The Dishes Don't Come Clean Use your meat thermometer to make sure the water is hot enough (130° to 140°F).

Check the various strainers for clogs and take a look at the detergent dispenser to see if it's releasing soap properly.

The Dishwasher Leaks Just like the refrigerator door gasket, the gasket on the dishwasher door can wear out or become loose.

Look for clogs in the inlet and outlet valves, make sure the clamps on the hoses are tight and the seal on the pump is good.

Make sure the unit is sitting level on the floor.

JOIN THE FAN CLUB Air conditioning is air conditioning but sometimes there's nothing like a fan to keep the air moving and the family cool. A well-maintained fan will last for years. Here are some simple maintenance tips to keep the cool breezes flowing.

If the fan gets a lot of use, dirt and debris will build up on the blade and the vents in the motor. If it's left to grow for long periods of time, dust and oil will mix

TREAT YOUR AIR CONDITIONER LIKE A MEMBER OF THE FAMILY

"What do you think would happen if you took a handful of dirt and shoved it into your mouth?" asked the friendly and blunt appliance repairman. I knew the question was supposed to be hypothetical, but as the mother of a child who had been an omnivore as a toddler, I really KNEW the answer.

"You choke and cough and gag," I responded.

"Well," he said triumphantly, "what do you think happens to your poor air conditioner when its filter is clogged?"

Of course, I knew the answer to that, chop-chop—the air conditioner gags, sputters, and even blows its condenser—which is why I was engaging in this quiz with the appliance salesman in the first place.

As much as I found him annoying, I have to admit I learned a lesson. Almost every appliance and electronic device generates heat, so it needs to take in air to cool off. Some of these vents have a removable filter and some don't, but they all need to be periodically cleaned. If the vents or filters are clogged, the appliance can stop working properly (if your air conditioner isn't cooling or your dehumidifier isn't spewing mist, check the filter first) or even heat up and die. Heed this warning—Clean Thou The Filter!

and form a gooey substance that ultimately affects the fan's performance and will, perhaps, burn out the motor. It's also very unpleasant to look at.

When you've got the vacuum cleaner out for the rugs, take the crevice tool and clean up the fan as well.

Use warm soapy water and a sponge to clean the blades and the grill as well as the case and other surfaces.

If the manual recommends lubricating the motor, follow the steps outlined in the manual and use the type of oil they recommend—usually a light machine oil will do the job.

SILENCE IS NOT GOLDEN— TROUBLESHOOTING A STEREO

There was a time when a person could actually work on his or her stereo or television set. But no longer. The components are difficult to take apart and taking them apart can void warranties costing you more money in repairs. Also, the cost of electronics seems to drop all the time and sometimes it's cheaper to replace something than get the old one fixed.

However, there are times when you can play detective and solve basic problems before turning the system over to the repair shop.

If your stereo has a hum in the speakers, check and make sure all the connections are tight and that the grounding wire is connected to its terminal on the back of the receiver. Also, make sure that the speaker cables are not touching the power cords. If all else fails, try attaching the grounding wire to a house-grounded item such as a metal pipe or to the screw on an electrical outlet.

HOW GRANDMA BEAT THE HEAT

We don't have a basement or attic fan to circulate air, but we also don't like to use the air conditioning all the time. I have found a way to stay comfortable most of the summer—I do what my grandparents did. I open a lot of the windows at night, and then close them during the day. I shut the curtains as well. If it's closed up tight before the temperature starts to climb, even a poorly insulated house will stay fairly cool into mid-afternoon.

Last summer, I bought a fan that fits inside the opening of a second-floor window. I turn it on when we go to bed and it cools the house so well that by early morning I often find myself groping for a blanket. Living behind drawn curtains during the day can seem a little quirky and Victorian, but you save some money on the electricity bill. Best of all, the neighbors can't tell what you're doing. You should be outside during the summer anyway.

Sometimes interference comes from other household appliances and will go away if you plug the stereo into its own outlet. Electronics stores sell low frequency interference filters that sometimes do the job.

If a speaker doesn't seem to be working, the problem may be in the speaker wires or the connections. Check the wires for tight fits and look for corrosion on the connection screws or clips. If the speaker still doesn't sound, jiggle the wires to see if the connection is loose or the wire is broken.

Finally, unplug the silent speaker and plug it in to

the other speaker's connections. If it plays then the problem is in the receiver. If it still doesn't play, the problem is in the speaker.

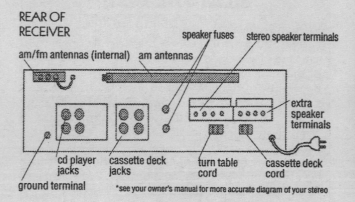

REAR OF
RECEIVER

speaker fuses   stereo speaker terminals

am/fm antennas (internal)   am antennas

extra speaker terminals

cd player jacks   cassette deck jacks   turn table cord   cassette deck cord

ground terminal   *see your owner's manual for more accurate diagram of your stereo

I CAN FIX THAT— REVVED

SAVING DOLLARS MAKES CENTS

TAKING CONTROL OF
YOUR TRANSPORTATION

The average family probably spends more to operate its car than to live in its home, but you can change the equation by performing preventive maintenance and simple repairs.

I used to be horrible about taking care of my car (I don't want to tell you how many times I broke down, but I think I'm the only person who ever earned a platinum AAA card). Then I came up with a perfect solution—I named my car. No, not a nickname (it's men who have to give absolutely everything a nickname). I mean a real name—currently I'm driving Martha, who joined the family after a tree fell on Yvonne.

The reason I named my automobile is that I realized that the only way I was going to remember to take care of it was to make it part of the family. As scatter-brained as I can be at times, I'm a whiz at keeping track of dental check-ups, annual physicals, vision testing, rabies shots, heartworm pills, and what seems like thousands of other appointments to which two and four-legged members of my brood have to be chauffeured. I'd always been able to work in a new cat, dog, bird or even baby—why not a car?

I celebrated my decision by taking Yvonne in for a facial and manicure (I mean wash and wax job). Then I sat down with George, made a list of all the things I should remember, like oil changes, tire rotation, shampooing (someone throws up in my car at least twice a month) and tune-ups, etc. I made the appropriate appointments, then entered the dates on the most precious of our family documents—the refrigerator calendar.

SUSIE'S HELPFUL HINTS

Make sure your dealer lives up to all the promises he made when he sold you the car and take advantage of any maintenance that falls under warranty.

Writing maintenance dates down did help, but what really worked was using Yvonne's name enough that all of us began to think of her as a family member. Soon I was reacting just as quickly when one of the kids said "Yvonne doesn't sound good this morning" as I did when they said, "Mom, I'm not feeling so hot."

The result: Yvonne never let me down and she was in tip-top shape until the oak tree sent her to the parts farm. At least I'm comforted by the words of the junk yard owner, who said lots of Yvonne's parts would be transplanted into other sick cars so their lives could be extended.

PART ONE

KEEPING TROUBLE AT BAY:

PREVENTATIVE MAINTENANCE WILL KEEP YOU ON THE ROAD RATHER THAN IN THE GARAGE

Automobiles are complex creatures these days and the time when Dad spent Saturday afternoon in the garage taking care of a "few little things" are, for the most part, gone. Not only are newer cars difficult to work on, they're very expensive. The money you spend on maintenance is a drop in a bucket compared to the cost of a new one. Increasingly, cars are being made to last, and proper care will almost guarantee a lot of happy miles. There are simple things you can do to keep the repair bills down but, short of becoming a mechanic, most major repair work has to be done in the garage. The more you know about the basics of automotive repair, the less likely you are to get taken by dishonest mechanics.

The best friend you and your car have is the owner's manual. It's boring at first but it has 95% (nobody's perfect) of the information you need to take care of your car. Read it and get to know it—you'll learn a lot about the thing you're more dependent on than good take-out.

Here are some preventative maintenance lists that can keep trips to the garage at a minimum.

AIR CONDITIONING SYSTEM

- Maintain the correct amount of refrigerant. Have it checked frequently during the summer months.
- Service faithfully as recommended by the manual.

BRAKES

- Once a month, check the brake fluid. If it is constantly low, a pro needs to take a look.
- Make sure the opening of the brake fluid container is clean before you add fluid. Dirt and debris are the braking system's worst enemy.
- Watch and listen for unusual noises when you put on the brakes and attend to them immediately.
- Once a year, the entire mechanical system, including shoes and drums, needs to be inspected by a professional.
- Inspect the parking and emergency brakes regularly. Adjustments are easy but the price of a failed emergency brake can be high.
- Use only recommended replacement parts.
- Make sure the mechanic checks the wheel bearings when other brake work is done.

ELECTRICAL SYSTEM

- Regularly inspect all the lights and blinkers to make sure everything's working. Get the kids to help so you don't have to get out of the car.
- Blast the horn occasionally but not to the point that the neighbors call the police.
- Check the wiper blades when you test the wind-

shield wipers. Use heavy duty blades during the winter if you get a lot of snow.
- Know where the fuse box is and when systems fail, check fuses before replacing parts.
- Turn off everything, including the radio when you shut down the car.

ENGINE

- The best thing you can do for the engine is to change the oil as often as the manual recommends.
- Always let the engine warm up a few minutes before you drive away so that the oil is circulating freely.
- Use only the weight and quality of oil called for in the car's specs.
- Make sure the person who changes it knows what goes in. Don't assume he does. It could cost you in the long run.
- Keep a record of oil use so you'll notice any changes.
- As the mileage builds up, parts wear down. Expect to replace things and try to do so before they actually fail.
- Don't turn on the A/C until the engine is running and warm.

FUEL

- Change the air and fuel filter every 15,000 miles or whenever the owner's manual says to.
- Use good quality gasoline with detergents to keep the fuel injectors clean.
- Shop around for a brand of gasoline your car likes. It may sound strange but cars do respond to different blends.

Just about the hardest thing in the world is to find a competent and honest mechanic (trust me, those are two different qualities). There are people who can fix anything on wheels but still love to take advantage of consumer ignorance. I used to ask my friends, but I discovered that they tended to recommend places that were the most friendly. However, I discovered I didn't like being stiffed by a polite thief anymore than a rude one.

I didn't solve the problem until one day I met Skip, who was also walking his dog. As the dogs sniffed, I discovered Skip owned the local oil company that delivered my fuel and serviced my furnace. Somehow the conversation got around to auto repair, and he said, "I've got the perfect place for you. Call my friend Otto."

Otto has since become my savior. Skip found him because he owned three service vans that cost him a lot of money and customer good will when they broke down. He invested the time to find the most cost-effective and honest auto repair, and because of his hard work and my asking the right questions I benefited by finding a great mechanic.

So here's my tip—you have a better chance of finding quality service by talking to local businesses that own small fleets of vans or cars. The emphasis here is on "small"—if they own a lot, they usually have their own mechanic. A solution that works for a competent small businessman will work for you.

- Have your fuel injection system and carburetor cleaned on a regular basis.

IGNITIONS AND BATTERIES

- Trust the recommended testing and replacement procedures in the manual and once a year: inspect and clean terminals, cables and wires, spark plugs, distributor, and all drive belts for wear and tear.
- Batteries need as much maintenance and attention in warm climates as they do in cold ones. Don't assume that because you live in Florida your battery will never fail.
- Don't "crank the starter" for extended periods of time if the car doesn't want to start—you'll eventually ruin the ignition system.
- Have an attendant check the ignition system before you replace a battery just to make sure something else isn't causing the problem.
- Try recharging a dead battery before you replace it.
- Replace your battery with one that has exactly the same specifications, even if it's a different brand.
- High-tech add-ons, like cellular phones, can drain a battery. Consider getting a more powerful one if you've entered the modern age of communication.
- Buy a battery with a guarantee that's in line with how long you expect to keep the car. Don't pay for a 5-year warranty if you're planning on selling the Dodge next month.

TIRES

- Check the tire pressure frequently because properly filled tires last longer. The manual will list correct tire pressure. Get a good quality tire gauge and learn how to use it properly.

10-4 TO THAT, GOOD BUDDY

Anyone who's ever been stranded in a car can appreciate the comfort of having a cellular phone to call for help (and to call a mate or friend for comfort while waiting). Unfortunately, cellular phones and service are expensive, especially if you have no other use for them. That's why I often recommend another device that you don't hear much about these days—a CB radio. These sets, which are normally identified with truckers, are very inexpensive and plug in to the cigarette lighter. Most law enforcement agencies still monitor CB bands, so you'll have a chance to get help nearly as quickly as you would having a cellular phone.

- Cold tires give accurate pressure readings. When the tires are hot the air inside expands.
- Check tires for general tread wear and for unusual things like bulges, tears and missing chunks.
- Rotate tires as recommended by the maker.
- The wheels should be aligned and balanced on a regular basis, especially if you tend to hit curbs or just can't seem to miss potholes.
- Have the mechanic check the steering system and brakes before aligning or balancing the tires.
- Use only the type of replacement tires recommended by the manual.
- Buy as good a quality tire as you can afford.

PART TWO

I CAN FIX THAT—

UNDER THE HOOD AND ELSEWHERE

Following are some projects you can tackle to take control of your transportation. The things you learn doing simple tasks allow you to tackle more difficult projects with confidence and skill.

REPLACING A HEADLAMP OR BREAK LIGHT If a single headlight or breaklight stops sending out those little rays into the night, it's probably a burned out bulb. If both headlights are out you may have a blown fuse, or a problem in the electrical system that will require a trip to the garage. Fuses and lamps, however, you can usually handle on your own. Take your trusty owner's manual and look for the diagram of the fixture assembly. On older cars the whole job is usually able to be done from the front of the car but newer models may require raising the hood or trunk to get to the lamp in question.

As always, refer to the specifications and get exact replacement parts.

If your assembly comes apart from the front you'll

PREPARE FOR AN AUTO EMERGENCY

I carry one of those giant handbags (some kid tried to snatch it one day and ended up with a hernia), and my family jokes that if we were ever stranded on a desert island, I'd have enough supplies to keep us going for a year. But as a woman and a mother, you never know when you're going to need a bandage, a needle and thread, a touch of lipstick, or a Macy's receipt from two years ago last Thursday.

Seriously, if you live in a climate with harsh winters, or tough weather conditions of any kind, packing an emergency kit is essential. In a box in the trunk, I keep all kinds of things I might need in any emergency:

- antifreeze
- blankets
- candles and matches (in case the batteries fail)
- emergency signs
- first-aid kit
- flares
- flashlight and batteries
- folding shovel
- funnel
- gloves
- hammer
- jumper cables
- motor oil
- penetrating oil
- pipe (24" to 36" for extra leverage with lug wrench)
- rags
- reflecting tape
- sand (small bag)
- screwdrivers
- spool of wire
- traction platforms (see part two)
- water
- wheel blocks [chocks] (to keep the car from rolling)
- wrenches

need a screwdriver—in some cases it will require a special head, but the proper item can be purchased at any auto supply store, and a jumper wire, which is a length of wire with an alligator clip at each end, also available at auto supply stores.

Remove the screws in the ring (or bezel) that holds the headlamp in place. Sometimes the screws can be corroded and won't turn. Spray them with penetrating oil and let them set for 15 minutes. They should be easy to remove after that. Underneath the bezel are more screws that are used to adjust the beam of the headlight—leave them alone.

Once the bezel is off, the headlamp can be pulled forward and unplugged from its connector.

Test the headlamp by connecting a jumper with an alligator clip to one of the battery terminals. Touch the other end of the jumper to the terminal or terminals on the headlamp. If the lamp lights, make sure there's no corrosion on the receptacle or headlight terminals and that the fuse is good. If the lamp is bad, replace it with an exact duplicate and make sure you plug the new one in the way you took the old lamp out.

Modern cars tend to access the headlamp assembly from under the hood and the lamps are easy to change. The catch is that they use halogen lamps which should not be touched with bare fingers because the oils will make the bulb heat up and explode. Handle them with a clean rag.

SUSIE'S HELPFUL HINTS

Make sure you carry enough spares of the necessary amperage to replace anything in the box with the correct size. Just like with The Three Bears, too much or too little isn't acceptable—it has to be just right.

Most headlamp and tail lamp assemblies are pretty obvious and with a little patience you should be able to figure them out. Just remember to keep track of the parts and screws.

HOSES AND YOU Modern cars are very complex and most jobs are beyond the skills of amateur repair people but, as I've said, there are still things you can do to under the hood to keep the repair bills down. One of them is checking and maintaining the rubber hoses that connect various systems to each other. Every six months or so take a look under the hood while the engine's cold and check for cracks, leaks and whether or not the hoses are stiff or spongy.

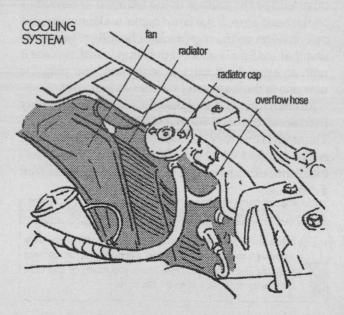

COOLING
SYSTEM

fan

radiator

radiator cap

overflow hose

Stopping Leaks You'll see that the hoses are connected to their terminals by a variety of different clamps from the familiar (remember PLUMBED) worm-drive clamp to spring clamps and screw tower clamps. If you find screw tower clamps you should replace them with worm-drive types. They're easier to work with.

SUSIE'S HELPFUL HINTS

Dip the ends of the hose in antifreeze. They'll be easier to slip over the Connection. And don't forget to slide the clamp on the hose before you slip it on.

Spring clamps are removed by squeezing the tips with a pair of pliers and sliding them off the connector.

The first thing to do with leaky hoses is to try tightening the clamps but if that doesn't do the job the hose should be replaced. As usual, find the exact replacement at the auto supply or dealer.

Sometimes the hose is stuck to its connection and you'll need a mat knife to cut it away. Measure the length of the old hose and cut a new one to fit.

Slide the hose onto the connection and work it up tight to the end.

Center the clamp on the connection and tighten it down.

DON'T BE CONFUSED Late one night I was driving home from a demanding PTA meeting and was stopped by a state policeman because one of my tail lights was out. I guess he wasn't in a very good mood either and I wound up with a ticket for something I should have checked as part of my maintenance routine. It cost me $50.00 to learn about replacing a 79¢ fuse.

One of the most important secrets in your car is the location of the fuse box. If you can find out where the little critter hides you can often save yourself a trip to the mechanic. Get out the owner's manual and seek out its hiding place. Take a look inside and you'll see rows of little glass cylinders with either metal or ceramic ends. Each slot is marked or coded for which circuit it controls and there will probably be some slots for spares. Sometimes a car will have more than one fuse box just in case you thought it was going to be easy.

As in your home, fuses in cars blow for a variety of reasons. Sometimes there's too much current, sometimes something weird happens that will never happen again, and sometimes they just wear out. It's also possible that the fuse was replaced at some point with one of a lower amperage and, as we know, replacements have to be exact.

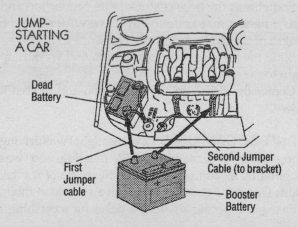

JUMP-
STARTING
A CAR

Dead
Battery

First
Jumper
cable

Second Jumper
Cable (to bracket)

Booster
Battery

Remove the fuse that controls whatever's not working and see if it's blown. You can tell because the little metal strip will be broken. If you replace it and the new one blows almost immediately, there's a problem in the system and it's time for a trip to the garage.

JUMP-STARTING A CAR I don't know anyone who hasn't needed a jump-start at some horrible, frustrating moment in her automotive life. While it's a pretty simple process, it still seems to strike terror into most of our hearts. Maybe it's the thought of all those volts charging around or just that it's a journey into the unknown, I don't know, but I do know I used to think the engine would blow up if I did something wrong. One thing for certain is that being able to jump-start a car can be a real favor to a stranded motorist, whether it's you or someone else. That's why jumper cables are part of my trunk tool kit.

The truth is, jump starting a car is just a matter of doing things in order and being careful.

Move the car that's going to jump-start you close but NOT TOUCHING. The cables must reach the battery terminals easily.

If you take a look at the jumper cables you'll note that they're color coded: Red being POSITIVE (+) and Black being NEGATIVE (-).

Follow these steps in order.

1. Make sure both cars are in Park or out of gear with the emergency brakes on and that the ignitions are both off.
2. Connect the red jumper to the positive terminal (+) of the dead battery.

3. Connect the other end of the red jumper to the positive terminal (+) of the starter battery.

4. Connect the black jumper to the negative terminal (−) of the starter battery.

5. Connect the black jumper to an UNPAINTED piece of metal on the dead car. An engine bolt is a good choice.

6. Start the engine on the starter car.

7. Start the engine on the dead car.

8. Remove the cables in the opposite order you put them on. Don't fudge on this, make it exact.

9. Ask the Good Samaritan to hang around for a minute to make sure the engine doesn't stall out. Let it run for a few minutes to charge the battery and drive it for at least 30 minutes before going to a service station so you'll know whether a charge will get the battery into shape or you'll need a replacement.

SUSIE'S HELPFUL HINTS

When you check the air, don't forget the spare. There may be nothing more irritating than pulling everything out of the trunk to discover that the spare is flat as a pancake.

CHANGING A TIRE Learning to change a tire was one of the most liberating events of my Fix-It life. The sense of freedom and independence was exhilarating and for once it was something I learned to do before I was stuck on a highway—I practiced in the comfort and safety of my garage with a couple of friends around for moral support.

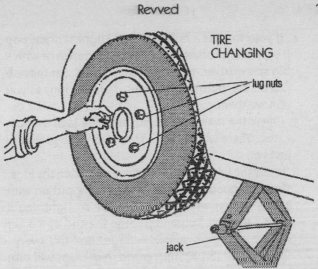

TIRE
CHANGING

lug nuts

jack

I'm not trying to say it's easy and that you don't have to be careful but I am saying that you can learn to do the job and it's well worth the effort.

This is the **CHANGE THE TIRE** drill.

1. Put on the emergency brake and shift the car into Park, or first gear if you have a manual transmission. MAKE SURE THE CAR IS SITTING ON LEVEL GROUND. IF IT ISN'T, OR THE TRAFFIC IS HEAVY, YOU ARE BETTER OFF WAITING FOR HELP.

2. Get all the things you need nearby. These things include the jack, the lug wrench, the spare tire, wheel blocks (chocks), a pair of gloves, and the instructions for operating the jack (See: owner's manual.)

3. Set the wheel block firmly behind the tire that's diagonal to the tire you're going to change. This will stop the car from rolling if the jack slips.

4. If your tire has a hub cap, and I hope it does, pop it off with the other side of the lug wrench or with a big screwdriver, to reveal the lug nuts. Set the hub cap on the ground near you to hold the lugs as you remove them.

5. Check the manual and position the jack as indicated. There will be a diagram. Don't raise the car just yet.

6. While the tire is still on the ground loosen the lugs. There's a good chance that they were put on with an air driven wrench and will be so tight you'll need a length of pipe to fit onto the end of the lug wrench and gain some leverage. Just like everything else in the western world, most lugs will turn to the right to tighten and to the left to loosen. As usual, however, there is an exception. If the lugs have a little "L" on them they work in the opposite direction. Loosen all of them enough that they can be removed by hand but don't remove them yet.

7. Now comes the exciting part. Slowly engage the jack, making sure you're clear of the car in case it slips out. The trick is not to raise the car any higher than it has to go to get the tire off. It isn't necessary to press hard, the jack will do the work. REMEMBER THAT THE HIGHER IT GOES THE LESS STABLE THE JACK IS.

8. Remove the lugs and place them in the hubcap where they won't scurry away. There's nothing more fun than searching for a missing lug nut on a busy highway whether it's pitch dark or broad daylight.

9. Set the spare tire on end against the car and remove the flat.

10. Lift the spare onto the lug stems. You may have to raise the jack a notch or two to get it on. (Remember, the other tire was flat.) Screw on the lug nuts in a diagonal pattern so that the tire goes on evenly and hand tighten them until the last turn on each one makes the wheel start to spin. The tire won't start to spin until the nut makes contact with the wheel rim.

11. Lower the jack until the wheel touches the ground and tighten the nuts with the lug wrench, using as much force as you can. Once the lugs are tight, remove the jack, replace the hubcap and put everything away. Then drive to a service station to get the flat repaired and make sure that the lugs are tight enough to hold the tire. If the spare is one of the kind that's meant only as an emergency replacement, have the attendant replace it with the repaired one before you go on your way.

ROTATE THE TIRES

Rotating the tires is the best way to guarantee longer life and safer driving. The more evenly the tires wear the longer they last. Experts have different opinions about how often the job should be done but I say it doesn't hurt to do it between 8,000 and 10,000 miles.

I've always had a problem remembering what tires should be rotated where—after all, they all look alike. So I number them with nail polish or permanent magic marker (you might have to refresh the number after a few washes or heavy winter) When I have them rotated, I draw a little diagram in a notebook I keep in the glove compartment that I can show to the tire place the next time I come in.

If you work carefully, think things through and don't hurry, changing a tire may not be exactly a breeze but it can be quite an accomplishment.

AND FINALLY, FIXERS—

FOR THOSE TIMES WHEN YOU'D REALLY RATHER NOT DO IT YOURSELF

BRINGING IN THE BIG GUNS OR, HOW TO HIRE A PRO

Here's a dream I have every time I'm trying to jam a zillion towels in a linen closet meant to hold nine washcloths. It's a dream of a perfectly planned living space with lots of room and lots of convience.

In real life, however, there doesn't seem to be a great-aunt or maybe she's lost my address, so my dreams have usually been a little simpler—just wanting to add a room, redo the kitchen or rewire the basement. And no matter how skilled a fixer-upper I've become, some of the jobs have been just too big to tackle myself. So, I've chosen to hire a pro.

TAKING THE LEAP

Just like there are lots of reasons to learn to do things for yourself, there are lots of reasons to hire a professional—lack of time being at the top of the list. So, on several occasions over the years, I've taken a deep breath and went fishing for contractors. Well, take it from me, the water's full of sharks out there just waiting to help you spend your money.

Think about it. You hire a professional to be sure that you get your job done right—someone who has building in his blood and a lifetime of experience. You want someone who knows how to do it properly and who will, for a fair price, make sure you get what you pay for and see that the finished job will meet your expectations. Not much to ask for—or so it would seem.

SUSIE'S PARABLE : THE CONTRACTOR OR

It's inevitable. You see some signs of mice, or you might even see a mouse scampering across the floor. So you go out and buy some traps and rummage around in the refrigerator for some old cheese.

You set the traps in some likely spots and forget about them. Maybe you check a day or two later.

Usually with a fresh set of traps you might catch a mouse. You strut and drum your chest and proclaim yourself the mighty hunter. You might even display your vanquished prey to your horrified family. Then you dig out some more cheese and set the traps again.

Next time you check you find the cheese is gone but there's no mouse in the trap. You reset the traps, but a few days later, it's the same story.

Then you start getting complaints from the family about mouse damage, or possibly even reports of mice casually sashaying across the bathroom floor in broad daylight. Your reputation as a great hunter and protector is, shall we say, tarnished. What's going on here?

It's actually a pretty simple case of priorities and level of effort. You have a lot of things on your mind in

But to find this professional and get what you need from him, you're going to have to enter an unfamiliar, possibly dangerous world in which there are more than a few crafty predators masquerading as responsible professionals. Only if you are successful at finding and managing a good one will you get a payback in quality and peace of mind and the satisfaction of a job well done.

THE HOMEOWNER AND THE MOUSE AND THE CHEESE

your daily life, just one of which is what to do about those pesky mice. It's important to you, but no way is it life or death. For the mouse it's a different story. He spends his whole life thinking how to get the cheese you so thoughtfully bring home for him from Food Universe. And, since he saw his brother cut down in the prime of life by the trap, he knows the consequences of going about it haphazardly.

The mouse studies how to get the cheese, because it is a matter of life and death to him.

It's the same with building contractors—you have the cheese and they need it. They don't need all the cheese you have, but they need cheese and they spend one hundred percent of their time figuring out how to get it.

The contractor makes his living and his kids' college tuition (and, if he's good at it, his deer camp, snowmobiles, sailboats and exotic car collection) from his ability to get the cheese from you.

Never forget, just like the mouse, he's the expert and you're the amateur.

THE FIRST THING TO DO Once you decide to undertake a renovation, the first thing you do is, go to the video store and rent *The Money Pit*. It's a movie starring Shelley Long (she's so cute) about a couple who buys a fixer-upper dream house and—well, I won't spoil it for you, but the name does suggest the position the movie's going take.

The reason you see it before you start is not because it contains many valuable lessons, or because it will warn you about the pitfalls and tribulation that you're letting yourself in for. No. The reason you see it is because as soon as anyone hears that you are hiring a contractor to do work on your house they will ask you if you've seen *The Money Pit*. Trust me, you want to be able to say yes. Otherwise, you'll get sick of hearing people you used to call friends chortling as they describe the hell the hapless movie couple go through. The subtext, of course, is that a fool (you) and his money (yours) will soon be parted. Trust me, it won't be long before you'll want to strangle the next person who brings it up. Anyway, *The Money Pit* is a movie. It's not reality—reality can be much worse.

But *The Money Pit* will, if nothing else, alert you to a lot of the scams and tricks that really unscrupulous operators use. Like:

- The contractor who disappears when the job is only partially finished, probably just after you've given him a substantial payment.
- The contractor who informs you when the project is two-thirds finished that the price just doubled and threatens to walk off the job if you don't agree.

A FOOL AND HIS MONEY

It is true, by the way, that a fool and his money are soon parted, and it is also true that this often happens to homeowners in their dealings with contractors. This can be frustrating at the very least, but, if that money has been carefully saved, or perhaps even worse, borrowed from a bank and is going to be earning interest at two points over prime for the next thirty years, it can be tragic. You have to be smart and you have to be careful.

* The contractor who won't respond to your calls, or can't be found, or comes to see you in a business suit to tell you that he'll take care of it as soon as possible after you discover that the new roof leaks like a sieve in the first hard rain.

THEY'RE HUMAN TOO, EVEN IF THEY DON'T SEEM LIKE IT

Building contractors are just people, and they come in the usual mix of good guys, bad guys and guys in between.

* The good guys are the ones you need to get your job done right. They are also the ones who, when you find them, need to be treated with trust and respect so that they will want to work for you and remain on your side.
* The bad guys are the ones who can make off with your hard-earned savings and leave you with a hole in the ground and a stack of soggy lumber.

- The guys in between—from those who are basically honest but can't resist temptation if they think they can get away with it, to those who are well-meaning but incompetent—are the ones you're most likely to find unless you spend the time to look carefully.

As you begin your search, don't have a problem with being described as "naive and inexperienced." People who try to pretend that they know what they are doing—because they don't want to be thought of as being naive and inexperienced—are easy marks for the contractor who specializes in gouging and cheating. Customers like that are easily led and don't ask questions for fear of revealing their ignorance. The lesson here? Get comfortable with your ignorance, learn to ask the right questions—and trust your instincts as well as what you know from your own experience and extensive homework.

The good news is that honest, experienced professional builders are out there, ready to do your project for a fair price, and be sure you get good value, too.

THE ETERNAL VARIABLES According to an architect friend of mine, there are four variables in any construction or renovation job—Price, Time, Scope and Quality—and all four cannot be maximized. That is, you can't have the biggest house for the lowest price in the shortest time with the highest quality.

If one of the variables is fixed—for instance, you have to be finished by Labor Day—then you will likely have to compromise on one or more of the others:

the price will be higher, the quality lower, or the extent of your project a little less grand. Know what you want and why.

WHAT'S YOUR BUYER PROFILE?

- **Price Buyer:** Your primary concern is lowest price and you are willing to make adjustments.
- **In-A-Hurry Buyer:** Your deck has to be finished for the wedding in June.
- **Space Hungry Buyer:** You have very specific space requirements for the project which must be met or you'll be forced to sell one of the kids.
- **Quality Buyer:** Your primary concern is highest quality. You've got the money for the project and want the best quality construction and materials.

THE STEPS Before you start talking to contractors, you need to have some sort of plan for the project. And you need to ask yourself a couple of basic questions. One is: how long do you plan to stay in the place you're thinking of renovating? It doesn't make any sense to spend a fortune on a home you intend to leave in two years. The other is: will what you end up with be worth the expense? If what you get doesn't really solve the problem that started you down the renovation highway, it wasn't worth the time, the aggravation or the money. You need a plan and you need to think it through carefully before you start talking to prospective contractors. It can be something you draw yourself, a standard plan you buy, a modification of a standard plan, or a custom plan drawn by a designer or architect. The important thing is to do your research and know what you want.

Spend time talking with people, reading magazines, browsing the Internet, going to the library, whatever it takes to be familiar with the technical nature of whatever it is you want done. The more you know, the less likely you can be fooled or influenced by a crafty carpenter.

Once you know that, it's time to start looking and here's a little sound advice for tracking down a good contractor.

SUSIE'S HELPFUL HINTS

Hey buddy, that window was supposed to be over there

If you keep track of the job while it's in progress (without being a pain in the neck) you can often stop a minor misunderstanding from becoming a major disaster.

- **BEAT THE BUSHES** The best way to find a good contractor isn't in the Yellow Pages. It's by WORD Of MOUTH. Talk to friends and to your trusted counter person at the hardware store or lumber yard. Try to get at least half a dozen names so you've got some means of comparison.
- **SUMMIT MEETINGS** Once you've got some names, contact them and arrange to meet them. If they'll let you see them at a job site they're currently working on it's a good sign that they've got nothing to hide. It's even better if they'll give you the names of former clients and encourage you to speak to them directly about how it went for them.
- **THE FIRST QUOTES** Once you've got a list of

choices, have them look at your job and submit detailed written bids (or quotes) that include materials and prices and a defined time frame for completing the job. Let them know that others are bidding on the job. It'll help motivate them to give you their best price. Don't hesitate to ask questions and expect clear answers. If they won't explain themselves in the beginning don't think they will at crunch time.

- **THE CREAM OF THE CROP** After you've narrowed down your choices to three or four, spend some time comparing the bids. If you've chosen well they all should be in the same ball park and all should have similar ideas about how to approach the work. Be just as wary of bids that are too low as those that seem very high.

- **ZEROING IN** Now it's getting tricky—making the final choice. It's based on a combination of your research, the right price and your instinct. Is this somebody you can work with if problems arise? Did you like the job they did on the Wilson place? Did the Wilsons? Will you tolerate them as they tear your home apart and fill the kitchen with sawdust? Do they seem eager for the job and do they understand what you want? Do you want them actually using your bathroom?

Don't rush the decision. You're about to start spending your hard-earned money.

- **AND THE WINNER IS** Once you've chosen the contractor it's time to really focus in on the details. This is close to your final opportunity to change your mind and alter plans without adding additional costs. Make sure the final plans meet your specifications and the materials and equipment list is complete. Be clear about what items are "owner-provided" and "contractor-provided." It's a horrible thing to discover in mid-renovation that you were expected to supply the bathroom fixtures so they weren't included in the bid and now the plumber is standing next to an open drain hole holding out his hand.

- **MAKING THE FINAL CONTRACT OR AGREEMENT** There are four things that must be in your agreement. Price. Make sure you agree on a price that includes everything necessary to do the job and expect the contractor to stick to it. Do be aware that sometimes there are circumstances that can surprise everybody and be prepared to be fair about the unexpected.

- **PAYMENT SCHEDULE** Don't ever pay the entire contract upfront unless you enjoy waiting for someone who'll never show up. Break the payments into a minimum of thirds.

- **THE FIRST** payment should be made when you sign the agreement and should cover basic materials and whatever labor the contractor needs to start the ball rolling.

- **THE SECOND** payment should be scheduled to come when the job is about half completed and you've had a chance to see that all work is being done to code and that things are beginning to look like what you expected. It should also be linked to a date. (For instance: by no later than June 15, 1997 the drywall will be finished and the cabinets installed.) This is the time to make alterations before things are so far along that changes would be time consuming and expensive. (Remember: if the contractor makes a mistake it's his problem and comes out of his pocket. If you make a mistake or want something to be different, it comes out of yours.)

* **THE THIRD** payment should be scheduled on completion of the job when everything is in place and working as it should. Ideally, a portion of the third payment should be held until the dust has settled and the contractor has complied with all the stipulations of the contract and, most importantly, *YOU ARE SATISFIED AND CONFIDENT THAT THINGS ARE THE WAY YOU WANT THEM.*

Make sure that, as the work nears completion, you and the contractor have agreed on what's called a PUNCH LIST. The Punch List contains ALL the items and tasks necessary to complete the entire job (including cleaning up and removing waste materials and trash). Stay on top of the list and make sure everything is checked off before you make the final payment.

SCOPE OF WORK It's important that you and the contractor agree on everything that's supposed to happen to complete the job, including quality of materials, level of work, and time frame. Also make sure that you know who's actually doing the work. Sometimes a contractor will hire portions of the job out to subcontractors. This is not necessarily a bad thing as long as you and the contractor understand from the beginning who is responsible for what if there are problems—like the roof is leaking or the toilet is not venting properly.

SCHEDULE You and the contractor should work together to come up with a work schedule, including a final completion date that's very specific—like June 5, 1997. The work schedule should be in writing. It should be broken down into phases so that you have some idea of how things are progressing and whether you're ahead or behind. Make it clear that any necessary inspections and permits must be scheduled, acquired, done and verified. Look for phases that can be clearly defined like: demolition finished; rough carpentry completed; basic plumbing and electricity installed; painting and finish work completed.

Finally, remember that an honest contractor stands behind his work, not only because he's a good guy but because it's how he makes his living. A contractor needs good word of mouth to keep his business going. Demand the best for what you can afford and expect to get it.

Good Hunting and Good Luck!

I CAN FIX THAT— GLOSSARY

ACCESSORY Anything electrical permanently connected to a circuit, like an outlet or a switch.

ADJUSTABLE WRENCH OR CRESCENT WRENCH Adjustable wrenches are an all-in-one tool for removing and tightening nuts. The jaw of the wrench is adjustable to any size opening and can be used for a lot of different applications. You just won't get as tight a fit as you will with a box wrench and sometimes they can slip.

BAR AND PIPE CLAMPS Used to span wide distances and hold things like a tabletop together while the glue dries. Pipe clamps come without the pipe which you purchase separately. Bar clamps are sold as complete kits.

BELT SANDERS Belt sanders make fast work of smoothing and finishing surfaces. Make sure it's easy to change the belts and the controls are accessible.

BEVEL GAUGES Bevel gauges have an adjustable blade that allows you to mark or copy any angle.

BORE To drill a hole.

BOX WRENCH Box wrenches come in sets of varying sizes to match all the different sizes of nuts in the world. Because they are closed circles with notches inside they fit the nut tightly and make it easier to turn. Ask for a 12-point box wrench set which will fit both square and hexagonal nuts.

BRADS Brads are tiny nails with tiny heads for tiny jobs.

C-CLAMPS "C" shaped clamps with an adjustable screw on one end. You simply turn the screw until the material is securely in place. They are used to hold large sheets of plywood to a work bench.

CHALK LINES Used to extend straight lines over long distances. String coated with chalk, usually blue, red or yellow, rolls out of a metal container. When the line is held taught and snapped it leaves a marking line. Very useful for making cut marks on plywood. It also doubles as a plumb bob.

CHISEL Wood cutting tool with a flat rectangular blade used to trim, shave and remove waste from wood. Chisels come in blade widths that vary from 1/8" to 2" although widths from 3/4" to 1" are sufficient for most needs. Chisels require practice to use properly but they are an essential part of the tool box. They are necessary for mounting hinges and setting locks in doors as well as cleaning and shaping wood. They need to be kept sharp and clean. Carpenters judge their peers by the quality and the condition of their chisels. A good set of wooden handled chisels makes a wonderful gift.

CIRCUIT A path through which electrical current can flow unimpeeded.

CIRCUIT TESTER A tool used by electricians to discover whether or not current is present in an electrical circuit. When the tip is inserted into an outlet and touches a "live" terminal or wire, the light in the other end goes on.

CIRCULAR SAWS Power saws with round blades for heavy cutting. They make cutting lumber and plywood a snap. With the right blades they can even cut metal. Using a circular saw safely and efficiently requires practice. They are great, but require respect when used. Use a combination blade (one that cuts efficiently with or against the grain for most applications).

CLAW HAMMER (16 OUNCE) A standard carpenter's hammer with a curved claw which is used to remove nails from wood and as a prying tool. The curve gives added leverage to ease removal. A basic tool for any carpenter's kit.

COMBINATION SQUARE A hand square with a handle that slides back and forth on a metal ruler. It is one of the most useful tools in a fixer's kit and can be used as a marking, measuring, and leveling tool. It will mark either 45° or 90° angles.

COMMON NAILS Common nails have round flat heads and range from 1 to 6 inches in length. For some reason they are designated in length by pennies—a three inch common for instance is called a 6 penny nail (6d). You can get a conversion chart at the hardware store until you get used to it. Used for rough carpentry.

COMPASSES Used for transferring very accurate measurements from one surface to another as well as, of course, to draw circles.

CONDUCTOR Anything through which an electrical current will flow. Usually copper or aluminum wire.

CONTINUITY TESTER An electrical tool consisting of a battery, a small lamp, and two wires with alligator clips used to test whether or not a circuit is complete or whether an appliance is properly grounded.

COUNTERSINK To drill a hole which allows a screw or nail to go below the surface of the work and be concealed. Used in finish work.

CUP Refering to bending across the entire width of a wooden board.

CUT FLOORING NAILS Flat nails used to attach floorboards to joists.

CUT NAILS Cut nails are made of steel and are flat instead of round. They are used to attach wood to masonry.

DRAIN AUGER The "snake" is a long piece of coiled wire with an attachable crank that passes through drain openings. When the crank is turned, the wire rotates and breaks up the clog. It's great.

DUPLEX NAILS Duplex nails have two heads and are used when something needs to be nailed securely but temporarily. They can be removed easily.

DUST MASKS AND RESPIRATORS We now know that some paints and adhesives are not meant to be inhaled on a regular basis and we must use masks and respirators as designated by the manufacturer.

ELECTRICIAN'S PLIERS Pliers with insulating plastic on the handles used for cutting electrical wire and twisting connections together.

ELECTRICIAN'S TAPE Black plastic tape used to protect bare connections and insulate them.

END GRAIN The surface of a board exposed when it is cross cut.

EPOXY REPAIR KIT An epoxy repair kit which can be purchased at any hardware store can be a big help in an emergency. Since the materials when properly mixed will bond to anything, it is a great way to make a temporary repair on a small leak in a pipe. Follow the mixing directions carefully and wear gloves and a mask. There are fumes.

EXTENSION CORD A length of electrical cable, usually of medium to heavy gauge, with a male plug on one end and a female plug on the other used to make temporary connections between tools or appliances and a wall outlet. Extension cords must be of good quality and rated at enough amperage to carry the load the power tools place on them. Brightly colored ones are best because they're easy to keep track of.

FALL A downward slope, as in the pitch of a roof or a plumbing pipe.

FENCE An adjustable guide for power tools like circular saws or jigsaws that allows them to cut a straight line.

FILES Files are used for sanding and shaping wood as well as taking the rough edges off metal pipes. They also can be used to straighten the threads on a stripped bolt enough to allow you to remove a frozen nut. You should have a full, round, half round, and flat. A wooden handle with a metal insert completes the set. Also called *RASPS*.

FINISHING NAILS Nails with tiny heads used when a nail must be driven below the surface of the material with a "nail set" to hide it. They range from 1 to 4 inches in length.

FLASHLIGHT You know what a flashlight is. You probably just don't have one and I'm sure you don't have a good one. If you do, I apologize.

FLAT BLADE SCREWDRIVER A screwdriver with a flat, square tip used for slotted screws.

FLORIST'S WIRE A thin gauge, flexible wire that is green in color and comes on a wooden spool. It is very useful for making small repairs of all descriptions.

FLUTED MASONRY NAIL Nails with spirals running down the shaft. They attach wood to concrete blocks or brick walls.

FRAMING SQUARE A large metal square makes sure everything's in 90° alignment.

FUSE BOX Also called the "breaker" or "service" box, the fuse box is the main electrical service connection and the point of distribution to the house system.

GENTS SAW An inexpensive dovetail saw (fine toothed) with a straight wooden handle. It is very useful for prescision cutting of all kinds, especially when putting in molding or making picture frames.

GLUE GUNS Glue guns heat several different kinds of stick adhesives and feed them through a nozzle directly onto the work. They're great but can get messy.

GRAIN The direction that the fibers run in a piece of lumber. When you "rip" a board you are cutting with the grain. When you "crosscut" you are cutting against the grain.

HACKSAW A saw used for metal and plastic cutting. Plumbers use them to cut pipe to fit. Unlike a carpenter's handsaw, the hacksaw is designed of a handle and a tubular metal frame to which the blade is attached, allowing you to use the right blade for the job. Hacksaw blades come in 8, 10, and 12 inch lengths. The teeth on the blade have to be harder than what you're cutting or they will dull quickly.

HAIRDRYER Use a hairdryer to heat certain plastics to make them more flexible and also to thaw frozen pipes before they burst.

HANDSAW A must just because you can't use a power saw for every job. Ripsaws cut with the grain of the wood while the teeth of crosscut saws are designed to cut against the grain without leaving splinters or tearing the wood. Panel or dovetail saws have very fine teeth and although they cut slowly, they are very accurate and do the least damage to the wood. I recommend a COMBINATION handsaw for general use. It will do a decent job of cutting with and against the grain.

HONE To sharpen a blade, such as a chisel.

HOSE CLAMPS These are ingenious little (or big) strips of notched steel with a "worm-drive clamp" that fits into the notches. The clamp has a screw and you turn the screw to tighten or loosen the clamp. You'll find them under the hood of your car to hold radiator hoses in place. They are great when used with an old piece of inner tube for an emergency repair on a leaking pipe.

INNER TUBE Go to the filling station and buy an old inner tube. Cut it into pieces and keep it handy for quick repairs.

INSULATION Material used to impede the transfer of heat, sound, or electricity from one place to another.

JIGSAWS Essential for fancy cutting and production work as well. The thin blade moves up and down as it cuts. With a simple change of blade they cut wood, metal, and plastic. They are easy to handle and if you purchase one with a variable speed motor, you have a very versatile addition to your kit.

LEAD PENCILS These are special carpenter's pencils that have wide flat leads which are good for marking and the pencil itself is flat so it won't roll off the table.

LEATHER GLOVES A good pair of gloves is important when you're handling pipe or doing anything that involves the potential for cuts and scrapes. They should fit well.

LEVELS Levels are essentially straight boards with inset glass vials. The vials contain a bubble and are marked with two black lines in the center. When the bubble falls between the two lines, whatever you're leveling is level. You'll want a small model called a torpedo and one at least two feet long, preferably longer for bigger jobs. Get models that have replaceable vials.

LOCKING PLIERS Locking pliers have a spring attachment and are made to lock onto the work like a clamp holding the material firmly in place.

Have the person at the hardware store show you one. They're indispensible.

MACHINIST'S PLIERS Strong jawed pliers for twisting metal and cutting wire. Electrician's pliers are essentially the same except they come with insulated rubber handles.

MALLETS Mallets are large-faced hammers with "soft" surfaces like cowhide, rubber or plastic. They are used with chisels and to nudge things into place that could be damaged with a steel hammer.

MASKING TAPE A fiber tape with little adhesive used to protect surfaces while painting or sanding.

MAT KNIFE Also called a razor knife. Mat knives have a retractable and very sharp blade that will cut almost anything. They're great tools, but *be careful*.

MITER BOX Wooden or metal jigs with saw guides that allow perfect 45° and 90° cuts. Used with fine-tooth panel saws. A miter box guides the saw blade to help you cut angles accurately. They're essential if you're cutting molding or building picture frames.

MITER CLAMP Actually two clamps in one, a miter clamp holds the ends of a picture frame or cabinet joint together for nailing and gluing.

NAIL APRON Used to hold pencils and nails, but it also serves a safety function. It keeps loose clothing from dangling over your work.

NAIL SET Nail sets come in different sizes to fit the heads of different sized finish nails. They are used to drive the head of the nail below the surface of the wood without damaging it. They are also called punches.

NEEDLE NOSE PLIERS Small electrician's pliers with insulated handles and jaws that taper to a tiny point. They are used to get into small places.

OPEN-END WRENCH These wrenches come with jaws on both ends and each jaw opening is designed to fit a single nut. They are sold in sets containing a range of sizes to fit most nuts. Because they are sized exactly, they provide a firm grip on the nut and because they are open-ended, they fit into tight places.

ORBITAL SANDERS Sanders designed for real finish work because the sandpaper moves in a circular motion and therefore won't scratch or gouge the surface of the work.

PHILLIPS SCREWDRIVER These screwdrivers are made with tips that fit into Phillips screws. The slots in Phillips screws look like a little "X." When the screwdriver is inserted it won't slip out. They're great.

PIPE JOINT COMPOUND A gooey material used to seal joints to keep water from leaking through.

PIPE WRENCH Pipe wrenches come in a variety of sizes from small to very large. They are used to grip pipes for turning or cutting and the more pressure you use, the tighter the wrench grips.

PLANES Wood smoothing and shaping tools consisting of a sharp blade set in a "block" of metal or wood.

PLIERS Pliers are gripping or bending tools with two parts connected with a pivot to form a handles and jaws. Some are fixed jointed and some are slip jointed (to allow the jaws to open wider). There are a million different kinds and, in my opinion, you can't have enough—they do so many different things.

POWER DRILL An electrical tool used to drill (or "set") holes in surfaces of all kinds. With the proper accessories a power drill is an extremely versatile tool, especially when cordless.

PUTTY KNIVES Putty knives come in a wide variety of shapes and sizes. They're great for filling holes, scraping paint and anything else you can think of.

RASP (SEE FILE)

RUBBER BOOTS Any plain rubber boot is a useful addition to an electrician's kit. Rubber is a good insulator and can help protect from electrical shock.

RUBBER COUPLING Coming in sizes for different pipe diameters, these handy items consist of a split rubber sleeve and a hinged metal coupling that fits around it. They are used for emergency repairs on leaking pipes but are also permenant once they're in place.

RUBBER GLOVES Sometimes you just have to get your hands in it.

RUBBER MALLET A rubber mallet or soft hammer is made of rubber, plastic, or even rawhide. It's great for banging things around that a regular hammer could break or mar.

SAFETY GOGGLES Clear plastic eye protection for when the chips are flying. They are important because your eyes are important.

SCREWDRIVERS A complete kit should include a variety of sizes and lengths. Make sure you have slotted, Phillips and if you really want to be serious, hex and square heads. It's a good idea to have a slot head screwdriver with a square shaft. If you're trying to remove or tighten a tough screw, you can fix a crescent wrench on the shaft to add a little leverage. A battery-operated power model is very handy.

SINK PLUNGER A rubber cup on the end of a wooden stick that you place over the waste opening and pump to create suction and clear a clogged drain. You've seen them, you may even have one. Just make sure the diameter of the cup is larger than the diameter of the waste outlet.

SLIP-JOINT PLIERS Pliers with adjustable jaws allowing them to grasp a variety of different sized objects.

SLOTTED SCREWDRIVER The screwdrivers with a flattened blade-like end that fit into the groove of a "slotted" screw allowing you to turn it.

SNIPS Basically beefed-up scissors. They have a spring in the handle and blades that allow you to cut things like sheet metal.

SOCKET SET (SMALL) Socket drives consist of a single handle with a rachetting nut which allows you to turn the handle without having to reset it on the nut, and a series of socket heads to fit a variety of nuts. A must for assembly of things like jungle gyms and work on automobiles.

SPRING CLAMPS Large clothespin-like clamps with plastic tips to protect the work materials, these clips are very strong and versatile. They come in a variety of sizes.

SPUD AND BASIN WRENCHES Essential tools for working on sinks and toilets. The large jaws are made to fit the special nuts used and the basin wrench has a pivoting jaw to get you into those hard-to-reach places under the counter.

STAPLE GUNS Staple guns use springs and levers to drive large staples into almost anything with maximum force and minimum effort. The electric or battery-operated kind make working with fabric or screening a breeze. But a good hand-operated model will also do just fine.

TAPE MEASURE Get a good quality 25' retractable metal tape measure with a 3/4" blade. The stiffness of the blade helps you measure ceiling heights.

TERMINAL SCREWDRIVERS Electrical screwdrivers with thin blades especially for the tiny screws used in many electrical appliances and electrical hardware like outlets and switches.

TOILET AUGER This is a snake made especially for toilets. It's shorter and comes with a crank handle attached to a solid shaft. There is a vinyl guard around the auger so you won't scratch the toilet bowl while you're removing the clog.

TOILET PLUNGER On a toilet plunger the cup has a cone on the end that fits into the toilet trap, making for a tighter connection and therefore greater suction.

TOOL BELT A third hand and a very convenient way to carry items you're using over and over again.

TORPEDO LEVEL A small level, usually 6" to 9" in length. A must for leveling shelves and checking appliances and doors.

TWINE Inexpensive and stronger than white string, twine comes in balls of up to 500' and is useful for quick repairs and tying packages.

WATERPROOF GREASE Lubrication that resists water and still keeps parts that have to turn in plumbing accessories like faucets running smoothly. Also helps keep leaks at bay.

WIRE NUTS Plastic caps with copper inserts used to make electrical connections. The colors of the caps designate the gauge of wire they fit. They twist on over the connection and are far more secure than electrical tape.

WIRE STRIPPERS A multi-purpose electrical tool used to strip the insulation off wire in preparation for making connections. They are also used to measure the gauge of wire as well as to cut it to length.

WORK GLOVES Essential when handling rough lumber or pipe, heavy leather gloves are great protection from cuts and splinters.

WORKMATE One of the great inventions—a truly portable workbench. It can be folded up and hung on the wall. The top is two thick pieces of plywood that become a vise by turning the handles at the base. Once you use one you'll wonder how you got along without it and it will serve you well until you're ready to build a workbench. They're sold everywhere.

WRENCHES Wrenches come in all different shapes and sizes. Adjustable and slip-jaw styles serve a wide variety of basic needs. You will eventually want a small socket set and may even consider a power ratchet.